YOU CAN HEAL CHRONIC ILLNESS

The Lotus Process:

8 Steps to Health and Happiness

Frances Goodall

© Copyright 2016 by Frances Goodall - All rights reserved.

The follow eBook is reproduced below with the goal of providing information that is as accurate and reliable as possible. Regardless, purchasing this eBook can be seen as consent to the fact that both the publisher and the author of this book are in no way experts on the topics discussed within and that any recommendations or suggestions that are made herein are for entertainment purposes only. Professionals should be consulted as needed prior to undertaking any of the action endorsed herein.

This declaration is deemed fair and valid by both the American Bar Association and the Committee of Publishers Association and is legally binding throughout the United States.

Furthermore, the transmission, duplication or reproduction of any of the following work including specific information will be considered an illegal act irrespective of if it is done electronically or in print. This extends to creating a secondary or tertiary copy of the work or a recorded copy and is only allowed with express written consent from the Publisher. All additional right reserved.

The information in the following pages is broadly considered to be a truthful and accurate account of facts and as such any inattention, use or misuse of the information in question by the reader will render any resulting actions solely under their purview. There are no scenarios in which the publisher or the original author of this work can be in any fashion deemed liable for any hardship or damages that may befall them after undertaking information described herein.

Additionally, the information in the following pages is intended only for informational purposes and should thus be thought of as universal. As befitting its nature, it is presented without assurance regarding its prolonged validity or interim quality. Trademarks that are mentioned are done without written consent and can in no way be considered an endorsement from the trademark holder.

Contents

Book and Client Comments v

Acknowledgements xi

Introduction 1

Chapter 1: Who is This Book for? 5

Chapter 2: Why Read This Book? 9

Chapter 3: Tools and Inspiration of The Lotus Process 13

Chapter 4: How to use this book 17

Chapter 5: Step 1: Acceptance and Surrender 21

Chapter 6: Step 2: Belief and Commitment 33

Chapter 7: Step 3: Self-Care and Inner Resources 43

Chapter 8: Step 4: Community and Support 65

Chapter 9: Step 5: Overcoming Blocks to Healing 77

Chapter 10: Step 6: Purpose and Authenticity 91

Chapter 11: Step 7: Healing your Past 99

Chapter 12: Step 8: Sustaining your Health and Wholeness 123

Chapter 13: Summary: The Lotus Process 129

Chapter 14: Wishing you a Miraculous and Happy Life 133

Appendix: EFT, The Enneagram and My Story 135

Recommended Resources 159

About the Author 161

Book and Client Comments

Book Comments

"In this powerful synergy of body, mind, and spiritual practices, Frances offers a message of hope, connection, transformation and healing. Based on extensive experience, and infused with love and divine feminine energy, she lays out a holistic, comprehensive road-map that points us to the healing potential available within and among us. You can feel better."

~ Deborah Donndelinger - Author of Family Energetics

"The Lotus Process is a step-by-step guide to healing. Gaining health runs so much deeper than we realise and on a practical and emotional level this wonderful book is all the medicine you will need. Moving you from what might seem impossible to what is possible, like the lotus you will raise and bloom despite conditions. Read this book and allow yourself to blossom and follow your joy."

~ Wendy Fry - Author of Mothers and Daughters: The guide to understanding and transforming the relationship with your mother

Client Comments

"I met Frances at the swimming pool of the hotel where we were staying and I was struck by her serenity and warmth and the casual way she said, 'Oh yes, I used to have that' when I mentioned the ME/CFS. She said 'I used to have that!' I thought to myself and this little light bulb went off in my head. She told me she was now an ME/CFS recovery coach and I asked her if she would be willing to give me some coaching. It was one of the

best things I have ever done in my life and I now feel levels of happiness and peace within myself which I never imagined were possible; not just recovery from ME/CFS, which was what I was striving for during those painful years, but a much better understanding of myself in such a way that I have also managed to successfully grieve the lost years of my life and make sense of it so that I can move on and be more fully alive in the world.

"After around 20 years, I can tentatively say that I'm well now. I have been consistently well for some time. It is hard to believe how hard I've had to work for this. You can't apply techniques half-heartedly without a level of faith and commitment to getting well. You need to be consistent and determined even when you start thinking 'this is really shit, this is never going to work... I've been too ill for too long/ I feel too sick to believe it's possible/ I'm too unsupported and alone/ here's another relapse – I can't take it anymore!' If you have ME/CFS, it's so important not to fall for the cynicism that can surround it. Whether it's that people don't believe you are ill or that you are cruelly judging yourself, or whether you believe all the blogs and posts which say it's about managing the illness, or you can never really recover or that there's no support. It's absolutely possible to recover and put it behind you and start afresh. I know this, because I did it myself. Thank you so much, Frances, for believing in me and supporting me. I owe a lot to you."

~ Zara, UK

~~~~~~~~~~~~~~~~~~~~~~

"I saw Frances regularly for over a year in 2012/ 2013 for EFT sessions, I also attended her EFT level 1 training. At the time I had been diagnosed with a small brain tumour; I was also suffering with thyroid disease and had developed some phobias and anxieties. I found not only doing EFT with Frances, but also learning it for myself, extremely powerful as a technique, and I would credit it as a large part of my healing. My brain tumour has decreased significantly, I no longer suffer with thyroid symptoms, and in 2015 I was able to conceive a baby naturally after being told by health professionals that may not be possible. I would recommend learning EFT to anyone, especially with Frances. She is extremely grounded, understanding, patient and kind. Although I no longer have EFT sessions I use EFT on myself any time I start to feel pain or anxiety and have also taught others to do so."

~ Lydia, Sheffield

"The short version of my recovery story is that 3 and a half years ago I was extremely ill: I had been bed and wheelchair-bound with CFS/ Fibromyalgia for about a year and had lost any ability to lead anything like a normal life. At that point my life had been reduced to basic survival. Over two years I managed to recover my health. At each point along the recovery path there were specific issues that had to be negotiated, and having France's coaching through that process was invaluable. After a very difficult period, I can happily say that I now have my life back. I'm excited about everything in life at the moment and positive about the future now that I'm well again."

~ Lawrence, Sheffield

"It was almost 9 years ago that I became completely disabled with MCS and CFS. After 4 years of trying all kinds of treatments and making very little progress with them (if any), I began Amygdala Retraining with the Gupta Programme and regained my health and my life! My healing was helped immensely through working with Gupta Coach Frances Goodall. She supported, encouraged and guided my healing process. In addition to coaching me on the Gupta techniques, Frances taught me EFT (tapping), which we used during our sessions together. I have been fully well for 3 years and enjoy a full work, family and social life. Frances' talents seem limitless and she is so very kind and insightful. I am forever grateful to Frances and Ashok for giving me back my life!"

~ Susan, US

~~~~~~~~~~~~~~~~~~~~

"I developed chronic fatigue around 10 years ago. I was working at a highly respected international architectural firm at the time. My role involved liaising with staff at all levels many of whom travelled internationally and would often bring back different viruses into the office which of course inevitably did the rounds. During a highly stressful period in my life of leaving my partner after nearly twenty years, combined with my system continually trying to fight the infections in the office the combination of stress and illness left me incredibly ill. I realised something was wrong when I couldn't manage to walk the 300 yards to the bus stop at the end of my drive.

"I would often spend days in bed trying to recover after an attack and the only way I managed to live something of a normal life was to sleep two or three hours in the afternoon. My hands would shake constantly and my legs would feel incredibly weak, not to mention the brain fog I experienced a good deal of the time. Planning was essential if I was to see a friend or had anywhere to go, and ultimately my life became more and more narrow and tied to the house. I felt in a vicious circle with it all.

"I began working with Frances and using EFT to look at some of the emotional issues regarding what was going on in my body and my mind. The sessions were a fantastic help and I realised the more I worked on and released unresolved trauma and baggage, the less I experienced attacks. There was something about Frances as a therapist that inspired me. I loved her compassionate and gentle approach and the way she was experienced enough to allow me to process my feelings and thoughts without the need to steer the session. I felt very held, and at the same time, had great freedom and range to delve into what was really going on for me emotionally. The fact that she had also experienced chronic fatigue was psychologically a huge help. I think the one important thing that helped me in my personal healing process along with the EFT sessions with Frances was that I refused to give the illness any attention outside of my sessions. I never spoke about it. If illness is a fire, I was certainly not going to be throwing the fuel of attention onto it.

"Many of my friends had absolutely no idea I was dealing with chronic fatigue and were shocked when I mentioned it years later in passing. These days my life and my health have changed considerably for the better and chronic fatigue hardly ever factors into my life anymore. I continue to have the odd session with Frances when I feel the need because, well let's face it, I enjoy the idea of thriving and creating the best possible life I can manage for myself."

~ Emily, UK

Acknowledgements

I'm grateful to my partner, Paul, and son Leo, whom I love from the bottom of my heart. I thank them for allowing me to focus some time and energy on completing this book in recent months. I thank my parents, for giving me the amazing gift of life and my sister, for being in my life since I was so young. You've all stayed strong, through my ups and downs, and have been there for me when I needed you, thank you.

I'm really grateful to the wonderful people who have supported me as I recovered from chronic illness and those that have supported the development of my work. I'm really grateful to all the valuable input of various therapeutic teachers and trainers, such as Connirae Andreas, Gwyneth Moss, Marion Rosen and Stephan Hausner. My supervisors, Rue Hass and Deborah Donndelinger, who bring years of expertise to help me continuously improve my skills.

We're always standing on the shoulders of giants when we bring fresh gifts to the world; I have so many people to be thankful for. Many amazing friends, mentors and teachers have supported my growth and healing on many levels.

I'm grateful to all the clients who choose to work with me as their practitioner to support physical or emotional healing. I learn from you all the time. Thank you for bringing your vulnerabilities and your strengths, and for being open to exploring the health recovery and healing path on different levels.

I thank Ashok and all the coaches at Amygdala Retraining; a wonderful and rich team of people whom I'm thrilled to have been a part of these last eight years. I'd like to thank my amazing friend and business partner, Sophie at Women's Wellness Circle. This work has met a deeper calling in me that feels so right, and I'm so glad to share this with you. I am also grateful to all the women who have joined the tribe, attended our courses and retreats; we couldn't do it with you. You have all brought so much wisdom and strength into this circle.

Finally, I'd like to thank everyone who has helped with the editing of this book; Dabney, Deborah, Moon, Paula, Hazel, Lucy, Rebecca, Lindsay, Rue and my dad (David). Thank you so much, you've all been a delight to work with.

Introduction

This book is for you if you have a chronic illness and have struggled with trying many different treatments and approaches with little results and long for a clear guide on how to heal. Reflect for a moment on what your life is like now, and how it could be to be fully recovered from the condition you have. Imagine how it would be to be fully well and to live the life of your dreams.

Many people will question, 'is there really a way to heal chronic illness or is it just about management?' This book will show you that there is a way to heal most chronic illnesses and a clearly defined path of eight steps to getting there. Once you follow these steps in the right way, it really is possible to experience full health, and to love your life again.

Take that in for a moment, breathe into that possibility. You can heal chronic illness. Despite what you've been told or might believe yourself, the potential to heal is a reality. Even if you don't end up fully physically healing, there is great potential for more peace and ease with what is. As you will discover shortly, indeed, this step often becomes the foundation for physical healing.

I had CFS (Chronic Fatigue Syndrome) /ME in my early twenties for 5 years. I went to see many practitioners and explored many different approaches to healing; most helped somewhat, but didn't offer everything I needed, and eventually I found my own way through to health. I discovered a process that helped me heal - I have developed that process for healing chronic illness into The Lotus Process, which this book will teach you.

Today I have a full and active life as a working mother and a lover of the outdoors. I've spent over a decade supporting others to heal from Chronic Illnesses such as CFS/ME, FMS (Fibromyalgia), MCS (Multiple Chemical Sensitivity), IBS (Irritable Bowel Syndrome), Endometriosis and chronic physical pain as a Wellness Coach, EFT Practitioner, Bodyworker and co-founder of Women's Wellness Circle.

Many of my previous clients had huge doubts about what is possible, but we worked with the doubts and they've stayed gently committed to the path of healing and are now fully well. I remember one woman, Michelle, who had so much doubt that she could heal. She believed that her condition was unique because she was affected by a particular parasitic infection that was impossible to heal. We worked with the doubts, she followed the 8 steps and now she is fully recovered.

I know from the inside out and through supporting hundreds of others on their path to health, that the body is amazing. Given the right conditions, steady and miraculous health improvements are a reality.

My wish for you is that this book provides an opening into the possibility for your own healing, and that The Lotus Process becomes a deep support in your recovery to greater health and happiness.

The 8 Steps of 'The Lotus Process'

Step 1: Acceptance and Surrender

Step 2: Belief and Commitment

Step 3: Self-Care and Inner Resources

Step 4: Community and Support

Step 5: Overcoming Blocks to Healing

Step 6: Purpose and Authenticity

Step 7: Healing your Past

Step 8: Sustaining Health and Wholeness

In the course of this this book, I will go into each of these steps. Throughout, I will tell client stories to help demonstrate points - I have changed the names and identifiable details to make sure they remain anonymous while keeping the essence of their story intact.

Chapter 1
Who is This Book for?

This book has been written for anyone who is suffering from a health issue and wants to find a holistic pathway to greater health.

The Lotus Process provides the possibility for you to take your healing into your own hands. It provides a clearly defined and thorough path to the wellness and health. This book will provide you with practical steps you can make to activate the healing response within your body.

Some conditions this book is most helpful for:

- ME/CFS (Chronic Fatigue Syndrome)
- FMS (Fibromyalgia)
- Multiple Chemical Sensitivity
- Electro-Sensitivity
- POTS (Postural Tachycardia Syndrome)
- IBS (Irritable Bowel Syndrome)
- Hyper and Hypo-thyroidism
- Skin Issues including Psoriasis and Eczema
- Chronic Pain
- Endometriosis

- Auto-Immune Illnesses

- Fertility Issues

- Insomnia and Hypersomnia

- Multiple Sclerosis

- Tinnitus

- Arthritis

- Pre-Menstrual Syndrome

- Post-surgery

- Anxiety and Depression

Many of the steps laid out here will also help you if you have cancer and are looking for a holistic pathway to health alongside any other treatment methods you are using.

For women, it could also help you to have a healthy pregnancy and birth experience, and through the menopause.

Mind-Body

Although physical illnesses have very real physical manifestations, the root cause is often emotion or stress related. The field of epigenetics shows that trauma in one generation can affect a subsequent generation, so even when we feel it was in our genes to get a particular condition, the root cause can still be emotional. Thankfully, when it is in our genes, I believe this is also reversible- we'll come to this later.

Who is This Book for?

This book is for anyone with any physical or emotional health label, as the steps described here have the potential to benefit anyone. Some of the steps may be more important for certain conditions than others; use your intuition and common sense about the order and the steps that you feel will most support you.

As someone who has recovered from CFS and since 2006 has worked primarily with others on this and related limbic-system conditions such as FMS, ES and MCS, this informs the process laid out here. However, through my encounter with other conditions people bring, in particular with my work with Women's Wellness Circle, where we get women with a range of physical health issues, I know that the process of recovery has overlaps with a whole range of chronic physical health conditions. As with all information, absorb and practice what resonates with you most and feels relevant to you and your unique set of symptoms, and leave the rest.

A Feminine Approach

This book can be beneficial for both women and men, yet it takes a more feminine approach to health and healing.

Statistically, more women than men get chronic illnesses, so I aim to bring an approach that helps to address some of what I believe to be the root causes of this, as well as to bring a more feminine approach to the journey towards health.

Did you know that women make up nearly three-quarters of the people who have chronic health conditions in the US?

- 5 million people with Fibromyalgia: 80 - 90% women[1]

- 1 million with Chronic Fatigue: 66 - 80% women[2]

- 30 million with IBS: 66 - 75% women[3]

Medical Disclaimer

Please seek medical advice and be sure of your diagnosis before following the steps outlined in this book. Many people have found these steps to be helpful to support physical healing. To apply to your unique situation please get professional medical advice on anything you are not sure about.

---

[1] National Institute of Arthritis and Musculoskeletal and Skin Diseases (NIAMS). 2014. *"What Is Fibromyalgia?"*
http://www.niams.nih.gov/Health_Info/Fibromyalgia/fibromyalgia_ff.asp.

[2] Very Well. 2006. *"Quick Facts About Chronic Fatigue Syndrome"*:
http://chronicfatigue.about.com/od/whatischronicfatigue/a/cfsfactsheet.htm.

[3] iffgd. 2016. *"Facts About IBS"*:
http://www.aboutibs.org/what-is-ibs/facts-about-ibs-2.html.

Chapter 2
Why Read This Book?

> ### Future Health Visualisation
>
> Imagine your life exactly as you want it in the future. Maybe in one year's time. As your fully healthy self, what would you be doing? What would you want your health to be like? Your life to be like? Visualise and feel it as if it is real now. Who is in your life? Go into your senses fully - what can you feel, see, hear, taste and smell? Embody the experience as if it is here now.

Take a couple of minutes to do the following exercise:

I hope that the above exercise helps it to become obvious why it is important you learn all you can about a pathway to greater health and gives you a flavour of what your life can be like in a healthy body.

If it also brings up some emotion about not having that health now, it is okay; welcome the emotion too. Allow the emotion to flow through you; it is natural to feel some sadness and grief about being unwell. Be gentle with yourself, give yourself a hug, do something that helps you relax, be it to have a bath, or to go outside and be in your garden.

Having good health helps make all of life more enjoyable. You can have more quality time with your loved ones, fulfil your life purpose and passions, and achieve your fitness goals. You can travel, study and have more freedom.

There are many wonderful approaches out there to help heal chronic illness and I believe the structure and approach I offer here are uniquely thorough. The Lotus Process philosophy is about helping to support not only lasting physical healing but also an experience of deeper levels of wholeness, happiness and spiritual freedom.

It is born out of my own healing journey, which has also been a spiritual journey, as well as my training, experience and work for over a decade in coaching, therapy and healing. It also attends to the healing of trauma, which was a part of my journey to health and I believe to be an important part of a deep and lasting healing for many. Below I share my story to give you more inspiration to read this book.

My Story

Between the ages of nineteen and twenty-four, shortly after I had become interested in meditation, Buddhism and Yoga, I found out I had ME/Chronic Fatigue Syndrome (CFS). At my worst, I was bed-bound for periods with severe mental and physical fatigue, headaches and dizziness.

I took five years to fully recover my health, with big ups and downs along the way. I explored many healing methods, including mindfulness, meditation, Yoga, Neuro-Linguistic Programming (NLP), Emotional Freedom Technique (EFT) and receiving bodywork, such as the Bowen Technique, to eventually make a full recovery. My need for awareness and growth was accelerated during this time, and I was stretched on all levels.

During my healing process, I was also found to have pre-cancerous cells on my cervix. When they persisted and got worse over a few years, I was advised that I needed laser treatment to remove them. I requested to wait six months to see if my body could heal itself. I continued with all my healing practices and added healing visualisations around my cervix, such as visualising healing light flowing through. When I returned to be checked six months later, they were gone!

Ultimately, to fully recover from CFS/ME, I needed to learn various lessons to be fully well again. Such as to honour my own feelings more and to communicate them. To follow my own path and purpose in life. To clear trauma and emotional blockages from my body-mind system.

Towards the end of my recovery journey, I began training in various healing modalities to support me to fully heal while developing skills to help others. The Lotus Process was born out of my journey to recovery and over a decade supporting others to heal chronic illness since I have been well.

I have had a full work life, as well as enjoying running (including a couple of half marathons!) and I have a little boy, Leonardo, who is three at the time of writing this book. If you want to read the full story, which includes the spiritual emergency/awakening I experienced as I healed, go to the appendix.

You Can Heal Chronic Illness

Chapter 3
Tools and Inspiration of
The Lotus Process

The tools in 'The Lotus Process' are likely to adapt and change over time, as I continue to grow and learn through further training and my work with clients. The tools and therapeutic approaches that I use currently in the process are:

- EFT (Emotional Freedom Technique)
- Coaching
- Meditation and Mindfulness
- Self-Compassion
- Expressing Emotions through Movement
- NLP (Neuro-Linguistic Programming)
- The Wholeness Process
- Structural and Family Constellations
- Hypnotherapy

For the scope of this book, I will not be able to introduce all of these approaches fully, but if you want to learn more about any of them you can find out more about working with me by visiting www.lotusprocess.com. On my website you can access a resource document with links to videos to support you with some of the tools and exercises, as well as information about how you can work with me at a deeper level.

Inspiration Behind The Lotus Process

My personal experience of healing chronic illness and all the therapists and approaches I worked with have contributed to the development of The Lotus Process.

Extensive work with clients with chronic health conditions since 2006 has been a huge inspiration behind the development of this process. This has been a constant invitation to clarify what I offer and to continually refine the process that is often needed to heal fully. This has encouraged me to be able to adapt to nuances in each unique health recovery path. To find the similarities in people's journeys, whilst also honouring the different sets of conditions that lead to illness, and the different approaches needed in order to recover fully.

I was a Buddhist for about eight years, from about 2000-2008. For the majority of this time, I practiced with what is now known as the Triratna community. I received a lot of benefit from this experience, and some of my meditations and philosophy introduced in The Lotus Process are influenced by my experience as a Buddhist, and having an extensive meditation and mindfulness practice for several years.

I trained in many bodywork modalities (Bowen and Emmett Technique, Massage, and The Rosen Method), which influenced this being quite a body-centred approach to healing. All my EFT

Training experience and becoming an EFT Trainer means I've absorbed some knowledge of healing chronic illness through EFT, which has influenced the development of this approach as well.

As a Gupta coach since 2008, I honour all I have learnt from Ashok's Amygdala Retraining program, the amygdala hypothesis, the retraining techniques and all the clients I have worked with from around the world who are following this system of health recovery. Amygdala Retraining specializes in helping people recover from CFS, ME, FMS, MCS and ES. Particularly if you have any of these conditions, I would recommend finding out about this program as you may want to use it alongside The Lotus Process - you can find out more about this program through my website.

With the creation of Women's Wellness Circle, a community of healing and support for women with chronic illness, we offer online events and in-person retreats. The approach and tools that we have embraced in Women's Wellness Circle to support healing chronic illness are weaved throughout this eight- step method.

The Lotus Symbol

The lotus symbol in Buddhism is a symbol of growth and evolution; the lotus grows up out of the darkness and mud, into the beauty of a fully open lotus flower. At any stage of growth, it is okay, because it is on a journey to be a beautiful lotus flower. So, wherever you are in your personal health recovery journey, it is okay.

This process is designed to support your growth to your potential as a human being, as well as to be physically well. I would suggest your deeper potential to be happy, free and with an open heart, living a life that is meaningful and purposeful to you. Many people who embark on a journey of physical and emotional healing experience a spiritual awakening as they do.

Also, to be clear, throughout this book, it's also okay for you to take on whatever I say that resonates with you, and to leave the rest. For example, if you just want to be physically well and the idea of the healing path being an awakening journey doesn't resonate, then leave it. This book can simply help you to recover your health, and that, in itself, is more than enough.

Chapter 4
How to use this book

Honour Your Unique Process

Although it is outlined in a linear, step-by-step way, the path to healing chronic illness is not so straightforward. You might have already done some of the steps, you might need to change the order, you might need to come back to some of the steps time and time again. In my work with clients I find that coming back to a sense of acceptance and surrender often needs to happen several times in a health-recovery journey, especially every time there is a dip in symptoms. This is not a backwards step; it is just what is needed to keep moving forwards to where you want to be.

Flow with the process of following these steps. Go at your own pace. Keep going. Get support if you need it - I'm here to guide you with the resources and offerings I have.

We are all unique, and our particular journeys to heal will be too. Some of the steps, exercises and suggestions in this book will speak more to you than others, you know you and what works for you. I give you full permission to be yourself as you follow these steps, and to trust your own way of doing it.

Be Mindful of Your Resistance

That said, be aware of the places where there is resistance to the steps or practices, as it could be a sign that you need to explore more deeply there. Parts of your unconscious mind could be working to protect you from something that is represented there.

I once had a client, Tim, who had a lot of resistance to facing anything to do with his past; he felt it was the past and had nothing to do with his present illness. Gently, over time, he opened to exploring the impact of his past. He discovered that the bullying he had experienced at work prior to the illness developing was a key part of triggering the illness. He realised there were still some feelings to process about this time. Not only that, but the incidents reminded him of his relationship with his father, which led to deeper work on issues with his father. Releasing the impact of both of these wounds from the past was a key to moving towards a full and lasting recovery.

Go gently

Take the steps lightly, not as something to add to a huge healing 'to-do' list; be aware of a part of you that might want to push the process of healing. I was working with a client recently, Maggie, who realised that she had been pushing too hard at her recovery and actually had to learn to let it all go. To stop trying so hard to do the recovery journey perfectly, but to learn to follow her joy more, spending more time in her garden, quietly enjoying the flowers.

I will weave this awareness and lightness into the steps, but it's worth making it clear from the start. You are not broken; you do not need fixing. You do not need to push this process. You do not need to do it perfectly. Just gently go through the steps and start to open as the lotus flower that you truly are. Your healthy and energised self is waiting to be realised.

The Lotus Process
Steps

Over the next eight chapters I will be going into detail of each of the steps of 'The Lotus Process':

Step 1: Acceptance and Surrender

Step 2: Belief and Commitment

Step 3: Self-Care and Inner Resources

Step 4: Community and Support

Step 5: Overcoming Blocks to Healing

Step 6: Purpose and Authenticity

Step 7: Healing your Past

Step 8: Sustaining Health and Wholeness

Chapter 5
Step 1: Acceptance and Surrender

"By letting it all go it all gets done. The world is won by those who let it go."

~ Lao Tzu

In this step, you will learn about the power of acceptance and surrender as a foundation for a healing path. You will learn more about the mind-body connection, and tools to help you access these qualities. We will also touch on the power of developing an attitude of gratitude to support healing. Naturally, this also promotes a healing response in the body.

The short relaxation exercise on the next page is to help you drop into a deeper place of relaxation, thereby assisting you in moving into a place of acceptance and surrender.

~Relaxation Exercise~

I invite you to read this poem and sit or lie quietly for 5 minutes before starting this chapter. This is a poem that my colleague Sophie and I often read out on retreats, helping us all to deeply let go.

Just for Now

Just for now, without asking how, let yourself sink into stillness.
Just for now, lay down the
weight you so patiently
bear upon your shoulders.
Feel the earth receive
you, and the infinite
expanse of sky grow even
wider as your awareness
reaches up to meet it.
Just for now, allow a wave of breath to enliven your experience.
Breathe out
whatever blocks you from
the truth. Just for now, be
boundless, free, awakened
energy tingling in your
hands and feet. Drink in
the possibility of being
who and what you really are
so fully alive that when you
open your eyes the world
looks different, newly born
and vibrant, just for now.

~Danna Faulds

Step 1: Acceptance and Surrender

Acceptance

We can't change something unless we accept how it is, for now. If we resist what is, we build up stress in our body-mind system. Any stress can lead to more symptoms. The more relaxed you are, the easier it will be for you to self-heal.

It's hard to accept an illness that has shown up uninvited into your life, with all its horrible symptoms and impact on you. But if you can accept what is 'just for now', a path out of this situation becomes possible. You might have heard it many times, but it's so true, 'what we resist persists', and what we accept can start to change.

We can even start to see that this illness has been sent as a gift to guide us back to a deeper place of wholeness, health and happiness. Bear with me here if this doesn't make sense to you yet; I'll explain more shortly.

Many times over the last decade in my work with clients, and in my own journey to health before that, I have witnessed the power of accepting what is, just for now. Once there is acceptance and peace about what is, the body and nervous system relax and health improves.

I had a client recently who was in a state of panic about symptoms becoming worse temporarily and we worked on her fears with tapping (or EFT, I'll explain more shortly). We also tapped on some underlying issues that she felt had led to the dip in her health. By the end of the session, she assessed her fatigue level as having gone from a 10/10 to a 0/10. This is a powerful example of how quickly everything can shift once we start to accept!

Once we start to accept what is 'just for now', we can start to focus the time and energy we do have on turning towards self-healing. Starting to learn basic meditation, breathing and relaxation techniques will help here. As well as time engaged and focused on doing things you enjoy, and being fully present in the moment, as much as possible.

On this note, I recommend cultivating mindfulness to support you in developing acceptance of what is for now. Being mindful means to bring your full focus and awareness into whatever you are doing, whether you are resting on your bed, cleaning the house, walking to the bathroom or taking a walk through some woods. Coming fully alive to your experience, your feet on the floor, the air on your skin, the movement of your body and bringing awareness into all of your senses.

If we can radically accept, including an acceptance that experiencing some suffering is a part of human experience, then we will be able to start the journey of healing. When I was recovering from my own illness an understanding of Buddhism helped me to find peace and acceptance, in the face of CFS symptoms that had led me to leave my newly found freedom at a university to living back at home with my mum and sister. Suffering is part of the human experience and yet there is a path to more freedom. Starting to understand this at a deeper level helped me to bring compassion to myself.

I am reminded of the 'serenity prayer':

Step 1: Acceptance and Surrender

'God grant me the serenity to accept the things I cannot change, the courage to change the things I can and the wisdom to know the difference'

Of course, I do believe you can change the illness and symptoms, but the first step is always a deep acceptance of what is now. I do believe it is possible that 'what is now' can change quite miraculously, but normally this requires some inner shifts and at least some of the steps of the process outlined in this book to get there. This can take a week, a month, a few months or a year. It might take over a year. Even if it is more than that, that is okay too; it is still worth persisting with the process.

Developing equanimity about what is, at the moment, is a piece of acceptance. Even though we might not always be able to change the symptoms right now, we can always change our reaction to them. In Buddhism, this is called the 'second arrow'. I've witnessed countless times the power of developing this kind of equanimity, both in terms of experiences of inner peace and in terms of actual physical health improvements. A recent client, Dave, comes to mind. Over a few sessions Dave went from a place of hopelessness about his health condition and his capacity to heal, to a state of gratitude for all the learning and growth that had come through the illness. This more empowered position enabled him to make a leap forward in his health recovery and to move out of living with his parents.

What can help with acceptance is to recognise that often chronic illness is teaching us about something that is out of balance in our lives and needs addressing. In that sense, the illness can be seen as a guide to deeper wholeness and happiness. It might be that we need to address a core issue around self-acceptance; it might be that there is trauma that needs resolving or it might be a way of protecting you from a difficult relationship or work environment.

It might be a combination of issues like this. There is often deeper intelligence beneath chronic physical symptoms that, once addressed, will unravel the symptoms and support you in regaining health, and realising a deeper level of happiness and fulfilment.

One of the tools that I will introduce as part of this process is EFT (Emotional Freedom Technique), which involves tapping on acupuncture points. The first part of the EFT process is to accept yourself for how you are now and with whatever issue you are working on; this sets up the body-mind-energy system for the tapping to do the work. One of the reasons we start the tapping this way is that you can't start to move through an issue unless you accept that it is here, for now.

If you're struggling to accept right now, that is okay; go gently. You can skip to Step 3 to help you build your resources further, and then come back to this step. Or you can go to my website www.lotusprocess.com, where you'll find a resource PDF with some videos to help you to move towards acceptance.

Mind-Body Connection

The mind and body are deeply connected. Even though we have real physical symptoms, more often than not, they are a result of ongoing stress and/or trauma. The symptoms can start

Step 1: Acceptance and Surrender

to resolve as we address the stress about the illness and any underlying issues. We can start to calm our own nervous system down, and to self-heal. I've personally experienced this and witnessed this with hundreds of people I've worked with, and you can do it too. Developing an attitude of acceptance and surrender with what is now will help with this.

We will learn more about the nervous system as we go through the book, but briefly to mention, we have two branches of the nervous system. The sympathetic and the parasympathetic. The sympathetic is associated with the fight-or-flight response, and the parasympathetic with rest-and-digest.

When chronic illness symptoms develop in a body, such as with chronic pain, it is often connected to the sympathetic nervous system having been switched on for too long due to long-term stress. Symptoms can also arise when the freeze response hasn't been processed through the body due to unresolved trauma. An attitude of acceptance, surrender and even gratitude will help your body enter a more healing state. Starting to experience this is a great foundation for the rest of what I am going to teach you in 'The Lotus Process' so that you may move towards a complete recovery.

One client comes to mind who had CFS and had made enough progress in two months to start back at work part-time, yet was not fully recovered as she still had some brain fog most of the time. We'd worked on fear patterns around illness, and got her into a more resourceful state. Then we started working on some underlying stressors that preceded the illness, and within another couple of months resulted in a full recovery.

The duration of this woman's healing process was pretty rapid, but remember however long it takes you is okay. Some people heal in a week, and some might take over a year. The length of time it takes to heal doesn't really matter; the journey is what counts. The more you can relax about the final destination, the quicker you will actually be where you want to be.

The mind and body are so connected that it's so important to believe we can heal in order to be able to heal; we'll come to this in more detail in Step 2, Belief and Commitment. We also need to believe we are worthy of health and happiness. Many people have core beliefs around a lack of self-love, and need to address this in order to heal. For others, it can be a fundamental belief that the world is dangerous; this needs to be transformed in order to feel safe to embrace a full and healthy life.

Surrender

What is surrender? I see surrender as the capacity to deeply let go and to trust, in something bigger than ourselves - and to feel the freedom and spaciousness of this letting go. We can have a sense of surrendering to a vaster intelligence than our small separate ego self. Depending on your belief system, this could be to your deeper wiser nature, to the natural environment or the universe, or it could be to Jesus, Buddha, a Goddess, God, or a representation of the divine for you.

Step 1: Acceptance and Surrender

In surrendering, a deep letting go can happen in your nervous system and trust in something bigger. Moving from an inner state of fear to an inner state of trust could be considered a foundation for a healing path. An inner state of trust is so much more relaxing and remember that any stress triggers the sympathetic nervous system, which slows healing down. Surrender and trust will help you activate the parasympathetic system, associated with rest and digestion, and an inner state that promotes physical healing.

I've witnessed clients' hearts being touched deeply as they let go and experience their vaster self. As they expand beyond their small identity, enabling a sense of trust in something bigger. Even with those who do not believe in anything mystical or spiritual this is possible, to expand a sense of who you are. A client comes to mind who is loving his daily walks in the woods, and clearly, has some kind of surrender experience while in nature.

Practices that support you to experience surrender include meditation, chanting and being in nature. Make surrender a part of your daily life. In this moment, see if you can let go of everything: all thoughts, all emotions and all stories. Surrender to a spaciousness that is within and around your body, the deeper truth of who you are. The awareness that fills your body, including from your toes all the way up the crown of your head and is aware of the space around your body. In this space, the opportunity for deep healing opens up.

Gratitude

Developing a sense of gratitude is a powerful ally on the road of self-healing that will help you to accept and surrender. Focusing on gratitude for what we do have, rather than focusing on what we don't have, can be very helpful. I witness when people heal, that they often forget how far they have come and instead focus on what is still not right in their life. I see their faces light up when they come back to celebrating the strides forward they have actually made, and really connecting to that.

A client, Sarah, comes to mind, who would often forget to remember how far she'd come, but once she could truly connect with it, so much relief would come into her body. It would enable the next stage in her focus to keep going, eventually moving from being severely affected with MCS, which led to her being unable to have anything new in her house and living with no furniture, to being fully well.

An attitude of gratitude as a way of being will also help, remembering to be grateful for a roof over our heads, the loved ones that we have in our lives, for the clean water we can drink and basically anything we can be grateful for to enrich our hearts and our experience. Helpful practices are to keep a gratitude journal or to regularly share gratitude with those close to you.

Gratitude Journal

Every morning or night, create a ritual where you remember and reflect on, or write down, five things you are grateful for about life. A list might look something like this:

Step 1: Acceptance and Surrender

- I'm grateful I have a lovely cosy bed to sleep in.
- I'm grateful I have a roof over my head.
- I'm grateful I eat good food every day.
- I'm grateful for my friend Sarah who emails me every week to check how I'm doing.
- I'm grateful for my son who makes me laugh daily.

Neuroscience has proven the positive impact of gratitude on our levels of happiness - it increases production of the two main neurotransmitters that are responsible for our feeling of well-being: dopamine and serotonin.

Gratitude for the illness itself often arises as you start to heal; you can realise how much you have learnt through these months or years of illness, and how it has supported you to grow. Countless times I've heard clients say 'I'm grateful for this illness now; it has taught me so much that I wouldn't have otherwise learnt'.

I understand that there might be some layers of grief to release before you can truly open to acceptance, surrender and any glimmer of gratitude at this stage. That is okay. You are okay exactly as you are now.

Before we move to the next step, I invite you to relax now. To take 10 minutes to lie on the floor and notice your breath, while practicing acceptance and surrender to what is now. Remember, it can be a powerful act, to make space to relax and let go into a state of surrender. You are so worth it.

> ## ~Relaxation Exercise~
>
> If you're feeling at all anxious or restless, I invite you to shake your body, do some stretches or go on a little walk outside first.
>
> If it helps you relax you might like to put some soothing music on before you lie on the floor with your legs and your arms out to the side. A position where you can comfortably surrender the weight of your body to the floor.
>
> Surrender the weight of your body to the floor beneath you for at least ten minutes, and notice your breath going in and out.
>
> Practice a sense of acceptance and surrender to what is, just for now. To help you do this bring your attention to the weight of your body on the ground, and move your awareness through your body. Have a gentle smile at your lips.

I suggest you do a relaxation exercise like this at least twice a day for a minimum of ten minutes while you follow this book.

Summary ~ Step 1: Acceptance and Surrender

The more you can let go into surrender, acceptance and practice gratitude, it will help you to build a strong foundation to support a health recovery path.

In the next chapter, we will start to explore the power of belief and commitment. This could seem contradictory to acceptance and surrender, yet as we will find, both are crucial on a healing path, you can't have one without the other.

Chapter 6
Step 2: Belief and Commitment

"The moment you change your perception is the moment you rewrite the chemistry of your body"

~ Bruce Lipton

This step covers the power of belief and commitment to recovery, and offers some tools to help you in those moments of fear and doubt to return to a more resourceful place. Taken in the right way, this step is a foundation to a steadfast and gentle commitment to your healing.

The Power of Belief

In order to heal, we need to believe we can and believe in the process or techniques we are using to support the process. I've done it, and you can do it too. I've supported hundreds of others in one-to-one and group settings, and below I share a few snippets of their stories to get you inspired:

"It was almost 9 years ago that I became completely disabled with MCS and CFS. I have been fully well for 3 years and enjoy a full work, family and social life."

~ Susan, US

"It's absolutely possible to recover and put it behind you and start afresh. I know this, because I did it myself."

~ Zara, UK

"These days my life and my health have changed considerably for the better and chronic fatigue hardly ever factors in my life anymore."

~ Emily, UK

"From a wheelchair with FMS I can happily say that I now have my life back. I'm excited about everything in life at the moment and positive about the future now that I'm well again."

~ Lawrence, Sheffield

A coach colleague, Angela[4], cites the determination to heal as a big factor in how she made a full recovery from a huge uterine fibroid and fibrocystic breast disease without surgery. In her healing, she drew upon her powerful belief that she could heal we well as the tool of visualisation. Within 6 weeks she was pain free and within a few months the scan showed the fibroid had shrunk massively. She hasn't had an issue for 10 years. Belief is powerful.

Neuroplasticity

The brain is rewirable, also known as neuroplasticity - 'neurons that fire together, wire together'[5]. We can create new

---

[4] Angela Caine. Transformational Coach. www.angelacaine.com

[5] A term coined by Donald Hebb, a Canadian neuropsychologist, 1949

neural pathways in the brain to support our well-being, relaxation and happiness. We have the power to calm our own limbic systems, or the emotional part of the brain, which also includes the threat response system. Knowing that our brain is rewirable can help us believe in our potential to heal ourselves! You can do it!

The Placebo and Nocebo Effect

The placebo effect is evidence for the power of belief. There are many studies which show that belief in a pill or person is paramount in the successful outcome of the approach used. It has even been shown that individuals who have received a fake operation in which they did not actually receive the surgery but believed they did, still experienced healing. I don't believe these kind of studies discount the tangible contribution holistic and alternative methods of healthcare add to support physical healing. It is simply evidence to show the power of belief, in addition to using a holistic health recovery program, like The Lotus Process.

Various studies demonstrate the power of the placebo effect - such as a Harvard study[6] that showed people with IBS improved by taking an inert pill, even though they knew it was just a sugar pill.

The nocebo effect is also proven to be true, that if we believe something to be harmful it more likely will be. This makes me

---

[6] Jo Marchant. New Scientist. 2011. *"Heal Thyself: The power of mind over body"*: https://www.newscientist.com/article/mg21128271-600-heal-thyself-the-power-of-mind-over-body/

think of certain clients that feel they might benefit from certain supplements for their health but are really afraid of taking them and having side effects. They are much more likely to have side effects if the fear is there, so we use tools to reduce their fear and help them embrace this supplement as a support for their system, which maximises the chance of it being helpful.

I read in an article thirteen years ago about a woman's healing journey from cancer, that there are three beliefs that are essential for healing. The three beliefs were:

1) To believe that you can get well.

2) To believe you are in the process of getting well.

3) To believe that the tools that you are using are working for you.

I remember writing these beliefs down and reflecting on them deeply. I would remind myself to come back to belief again and again, and sometimes to get there I would need to release some sadness about the fact that I'd just had another big health dip. I realised when it came to healing, my mindset could become a powerful ally.

EFT and 'A Pause' are tools from The Lotus Process we can use to help release our fears and doubts about being able to heal, which we will come to soon. The more you can come back to a place of trust, the quicker you will heal. I've witnessed this time and time again with clients.

Step 2: Belief and Commitment

In the exercise described on the next page many clients start with about a 5/10 belief in recovery. When I ask 'what stops it from being a 10?' I have had clients tell me, for example: 'I've been ill for so long', 'I've tried so many things to heal, it's not safe to get my hopes up now', 'my doctor told me I would never recover', 'my nervous system is just too sensitive' or 'my mum has it and she's still ill'. We then tap or do other processes to work through each aspect, until by the end of the session they usually get to a 9 or 10/10 belief. This is a practice you can keep coming back to as you heal, whenever doubt arises, to keep the belief there in the heart of it all, that you can do this.

~EFT to Overcome Doubts Exercise~

Say to yourself 'I can fully recover my health' and check-in how much out of 10 you believe it to be true. 10 being 100%, and 0 being not at all. Guess if you are not sure.

What stops it being a 10? Journal on underlying beliefs, fears, emotions and thoughts.

Pick one of the limiting beliefs, feelings or thoughts. Give this a score out of 10 for how much you believe it to be true or how bothersome the emotions are to you now.

Find a statement of acceptance of yourself with the issue e.g. 'Even though I've been unwell for so long and I've tried so many things to heal I accept myself anyway'.

Tap the 'karate chop point' (see the diagram on the next page) on the side of your hand three times while repeating the affirmation.

Tap around all the points on the body (see the diagram on the next page) while repeating what the issue is 'I've been unwell for so long and I've tried so many things to heal'

Give this aspect a rating out of 10 again, keep tapping until you bring it down

Tap on the remaining aspects of this belief and bring the intensity of each one down to a 0 or a 1 ideally.

Check-in with 'I can fully recover my health' again and give it a rating out of 10.

See the next page to find out where the tapping points are and the appendix for a more thorough introduction to the EFT process.

Step 2: Belief and Commitment

EFT Tapping Points

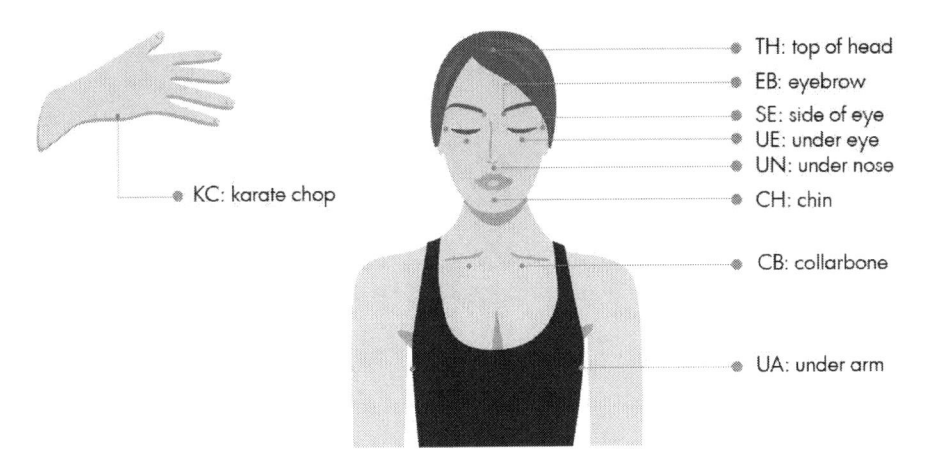

- TH: top of head
- EB: eyebrow
- SE: side of eye
- UE: under eye
- UN: under nose
- KC: karate chop
- CH: chin
- CB: collarbone
- UA: under arm

Chart courtesy of Gillian Morris Coaching (Designed by Love at home design)

Power of Visualisation

Visualisation is another powerful tool to help you to develop the belief that you can heal and the commitment to keep going through the ups and downs. The brain doesn't know the difference between what's real and what's imagined, so if you visualise health regularly it actually helps you to get there. As I mentioned in my story at the beginning, I believe visualisation of healing light flowing into my cervix was one of the practices that helped the pre-cancerous cells that were there to heal. The exercise on the next page is another way of practicing visualisation to support you to heal physically.

> ## ~Visualise and Embody Health Exercise~
>
> Take about 5-15 minutes for this practice
>
> Get into a comfortable sitting or lying position.
>
> Start to imagine life exactly as you want it in the future. Maybe in 6 months, in a year or even in three years'. What would you want your health and your life to be like?
>
> Visualize and/or feel it as if it is real now. What would you be doing, who are you, who is in your life, as your fully well self? Go into your senses fully, what can you feel, see, hear, taste and smell? Embody the experience as if it is here now.
>
> If there was a light that helped you embody this experience, would it have a colour? Visualise a white or coloured light flowing into the crown of your head and filling you up, cleaning away anything in your body-mind system that is in the way of your future healthy self emerging.
>
> Journal about what you felt, saw and experienced

Practice this visualisation on a daily basis, or at least three times a week, to help you to stay motivated on your path and also to help health become a reality for you. Go to www.lotusprocess.com where there's a free resources PDF including a link for a short video of a guided health visualisation.

Summary ~ Step 2: Belief and Commitment

Hopefully, as you've gone through this chapter you've started to get the power of belief to support you in healing, and committing to your path to wellbeing. You can heal chronic illness. YOU CAN do it. This will set you up well for committing to the next step more fully, on building your inner resources to support you in healing.

Chapter 7
Step 3: Self-Care and Inner Resources

"Close your eyes and follow your breath

to the still place that leads

to the invisible path

that leads you home."

~St Theresa of Avila

There are so many ways to take care of yourself and build your resources, so this step is a long one. We will be exploring how to build your internal resources, including learning how to look after your physical body, to develop your compassionate self, build your self-care routine, regulate your nervous system and more. I recommend following your joy with this, take what resonates, and leave the rest. One of the foundations of this step is to look after your body with good sleep, to eat well and exercise as much as possible for where you are with your health.

Sleep

I recommend moving towards a sleep routine of what a healthy person would be, meaning early-ish nights (between 9-11pm) and early-ish mornings (7am-9am). A routine that enables you to have at least 7-8 hours of sleep a night and to be able to have a full morning. Many of my clients have found themselves in a routine in which they sleep from say 2am-11am. Some even experience a complete reversal of sleeping in the day and being awake at night. When I was unwell I got into a less healthy routine of say 12pm-10am. It was a breakthrough for me when I changed this through working with a psychologist.

If you agree and want to change your sleep routine, go gently, moving slowly towards a healthier person's routine. A recent client said this felt like a breakthrough as she had more time to do all her self-care practices in the morning, and still have some time in the morning for other things.

I highly recommend winding down slowly every evening, with dim lighting and no screens at least an hour before bed to help the sleep inducing hormone melatonin to be released. If you are still struggling with sleep after following the basics of winding down slowly at night and using tools to help release fears and thoughts about not sleeping, then get additional support with this. Improving sleep is an area I can help with further in my more in-depth support options.

Improving your sleep is a foundation for good health, recent studies show that insomnia can cause various health conditions such as anxiety and depression, heart disease and diabetes[7]. I would suggest, though, that deep relaxation and meditation can have a similar impact on your health and wellness. If you are struggling to sleep, allow yourself to deeply relax and surrender, and your system will be restored.

---

[7] Express. 2016. *"Lack of sleep can lead to killer conditions"*: http://www.express.co.uk/life-style/health/663612/Lack-sleep-deprivation-killer-conditions-insomnia.

Nutrition

I recommend a basic good diet, such as lots of vegetables, good quality protein and carbohydrates. I also recommend green smoothies or juices as a way of getting lots of minerals and vitamins into your body that are easy to digest. You might find it beneficial to cut out or down on dairy, wheat, caffeine and sugar. At least while you recover your health. These are all substances that many people struggle to digest, can lower the immune system or put some stress on a system that is already overloaded.

These are all simple ways we can help to create a physical foundation for health in the body. I don't recommend getting into extensive and expensive supplement routines, or allowing diet to become a source of stress. It might be better to let the good diet go at times than for it to become a source of stress.

Supplements that might be helpful, that I have used as I healed, are spirulina, probiotics, magnesium and vitamin D. Getting good probiotics daily is meant to be a great way of promoting good health and ideally through natural sources like live yoghurt, fermented vegetable, kefir or kombucha.

Exercise

In terms of exercise, I recommend healing practices like yoga, chi kung or T'ai Chi. I also recommend walking in nature, swimming and building up aerobic activity gradually. Perhaps starting with walking or swimming, and at a level that is safe for you at this time in your recovery journey. Gradually building up, while following all the other steps and tools this book introduces to you. The more deeply you are calming your system down and promoting self-healing, the safer it will be to build up your exercise.

Self-Care

You need to build a really positive self-care routine into your life. I recommend, when you first get up, before or after a shower, to practice some gentle movement such as some yoga or chi kung, followed by some meditation. If you can start the day right, it really helps the rest of the day to flow with more ease and the possibility for energy and joy to be experienced. Ongoing self-care is also a foundational prerequisite of any healing path, and sustaining health once you are well.

Meditation

Meditation is a life-long tool for health and happiness. Dwelling in stillness and looking inward for some part of each day, you can touch what is most real in yourself, and often undeveloped. When you can be centred, even for brief periods of time, in the face of the pull of the outer world, you can be at home wherever you find yourself. You're not having to look elsewhere for something to fill you up or make you happy. You can be at peace with things as they are, moment by moment.

There are several different kinds of meditation we can do. A good place to start is with the breath. Simply spending 5-40 minutes focusing awareness on the breath as it goes in and out.

Over time this helps you to still the mind and enter a state of deeper concentration. It is also a process of noticing thoughts that come and go, or take your focus away from the breath, and to keep coming back to the breath again and again. Some people find using counting a helpful way to anchor attention on the breath, such as counting from 1 to 10, a new number on each in breath, and once you reach 10, returning to 1 again.

Another form of meditation is focusing on the heart and wishing yourself and others well, you will come to a practice of this in Step 5, Overcoming Blocks to Healing. This can be a powerful way to deepen into self-acceptance and to transform blocks to healing.

All methods encourage the mind to be absorbed in the focus of the meditation, thereby assisting a stilling of the mind and being. I recommend reading books on meditation to find out more or joining a local class, listening to guided meditations, going on a retreat or joining an online group. For a guided meditation with me visit my website.

Regular meditation in the day will help to calm your system and 'taking short breaks to meditate can help refresh, recharge and "reboot" the brain'[8]. In this sense, regular meditation helps you to have more energy and to need less sleep at night.

---

[8] Mathew. B. James, Psychology Today. 2011. *"Sleep, Cycles and Rebooting Your Brain with Meditation"*:
https://www.psychologytoday.com/blog/focus-forgiveness/201112/sleep-cycles-and-rebooting-your-brain-meditation.

Walking Meditation

You can also meditate while walking. To begin, become fully aware as one foot connects with the ground, the heel comes down first and then the toe. Feel the shift in the weight and as the other foot is lifting and moving ahead and then heel and toe down in turn. Continue only focusing on the feet and the experience of walking.

As with all other methods of meditation, when the mind wanders away from the feet and the experience of walking, bring it back to each step. You are cultivating the felt sensation of walking, nothing more. The head may condemn the exercise, or play games or try to distract you. Just return to your feet and walking with awareness. You can practice this at any time, when walking to the shops or in nature.

"Walk as if you are kissing the Earth with your feet."

~ Thich Nhat Hanh

Mindfulness

Mindfulness is practicing moment to moment awareness of what is. We can learn to become increasingly aware of how we feel (physically and emotionally), how we move and how we respond to each moment in life. It's not always possible or easy to change how things are in the present, but we can always change how we respond to the ways things are.

Mindfulness enables us to live our life from a more centred place, where the passing thoughts, sensations and emotions can be experienced from a still centre of awareness. Whether we are sitting in meditation, doing the washing up, out with friends or stuck in a traffic jam, the opportunity to practice mindfulness is always there.

By practicing mindfulness, we can transform and enrich our lives. Each moment we have the chance to come to a place of awareness and stillness within ourselves, and that for me is amazing! Without meditation and mindfulness, I can't imagine having recovered from Chronic Fatigue; it was an integral part of that journey.

I have many memories of the power of these practices, which benefit me in the here and now as I write these words and I am simply present with the keyboard, and the sound of the birds outside. I smile and feel a deep peace and stillness within.

The possibility for present moment awareness is always there in all of us, once the mud has settled. Meditation is proven to calm the nervous system and help you enter deeper brainwave patterns that support the activation of the parasympathetic nervous system and physical healing.

Regular Pockets of Self-Care

Throughout the day coming back to pockets of self-care is a very supportive practice for healing chronic illness. This might mean pausing every 30 minutes for 5 minutes of breathing or stretching, a 20-minute meditation before lunch and a 30-minute gentle walk in nature in the afternoon.

If you notice a pattern of thoughts about symptoms, or thoughts that are not serving you in being at peace or happy, I recommend using 'A Pause' Exercise practice or EFT for a direct way of starting to use the tools to self-regulate your own nervous system.

We all have within ourselves the capacity for self-acceptance, for wholeness, even for self-love. This can be cultivated within us by practices such as loving-kindness meditation, The Wholeness Process, A Pause, NLP and others. As we develop this within ourselves, the quicker our nervous systems will heal and the more resources we will have to work with core issues.

Make that Decision!

Neuroscience has proven that dwelling on decisions does not increase happiness. If you find yourself doing this, use mindfulness, meditation and pausing to support you in making a clear decision.

Working on your self-acceptance and love will help you get better at making a decision, as regular indecision can be a sign of low self-esteem. Often if you create space to acknowledge the two parts of you involved that perhaps want different things and what these two parts want, it will help you come to a clearer decision. I had a client, Mike, who recently found this practice to be really helpful with a decision that was draining his energy. After doing this, he was clear on which pathway to take, and his health started to improve again.

Developing Self-Love

As well as a supportive community (which is the next step of this process) a deeper sense of support can also come through contacting self-love. According to most spiritual traditions, mystics, saints and enlightened beings, our deeper nature is love. Developing your connection with the wellspring of love within your heart will help you connect with your deeper self and the source of all life.

I recommend developing your connection with the love in the core of you. This will help you to recognise where human relationships can go wrong and where the remedy could be. In a sense, you can start to feel supported by the source of everything (love, God, the universe, nature or whatever you want to call it). To develop this sense of connection and self-love it helps to meditate and/or pray, do yoga, spend time in nature and also to be around other people who have this approach to life. I love this expression of the love at the heart of you, from John Welwood:

"I would define love very simply: a potent blend of openness and warmth, which allows us to make real contact, to take delight in and appreciate, and to be at one with- ourselves, others and life itself. Openness- the heart's pure, unconditional yes- is love's essence. And warmth is love's basic expression, arising as a natural extension of this yes- the desire to reach out and touch, connect with, and nourish what we love. If love's openness is like the clear cloudless sky, its warmth is like the sunlight streaming through that sky,

emitting a rainbow-like spectrum of colours: passion, joy, contact, communion, kindness, caring, understanding, service, dedication, and devotion, to name just a few." [9]

Nature and Grounding

Finally, in terms of building resources, I can't highlight enough the power of spending time in nature. Eve Ensler[10] credits part of her recovery from cancer to seeing a tree outside of the window of the hospital. Studies have shown the power trees and nature scenes can have on healing, such as one that showed:

"the patients with a tree view had shorter postoperative hospital stays, had fewer negative evaluative comments from nurses, took fewer moderate and strong analgesic doses, and had slightly lower scores for minor post-surgical complications" [11]

Get out in your garden every day if you have one, or to a local park or woods. Walk in nature every day if possible. Literally, I feel like I am being fed by the trees when I make time for this these days, I can feel my cells and whole system being revitalised. I have many clients tell me that once they can get out into nature, it becomes a deep resource of support for their healing. Some start in the garden and then move onto walks outdoors.

---

[9] Welwood, J (2007). *Perfect Love, Imperfect Relationships.* Shambhala Publications, Inc

[10] Ensler, E of the (2001) *'The Vagina Monologues',* Virago

[11] Ulrich, R.S. Science. New Series. Volume 224. Issue 4647 (Apr. 27, 1984), 420-421. *"View through a Window May Influence Recovery from Surgery":* https://mdc.mo.gov/sites/default/files/resources/2012/10/ulrich.pdf

Step 3: Self-Care and Inner Resources

Take time every day to be in nature if you can, and ideally get your bare feet on the ground, and lean up against a tree. This is a powerful way to connect with the earth and experience the healing benefits of doing so. When I was unwell, I would often spend time with trees and today it is a way I keep myself grounded and strong, especially as I spend a lot of time working on a computer.

Sometimes when nothing makes sense, and your energy is in a mess, having your bare feet on the ground and your body leant up against a tree is the most potent medicine for you. One study[12] sites:

"Emerging scientific research supports the concept that the Earth's electrons induce multiple physiological changes of clinical significance, including reduced pain, better sleep, a shift from sympathetic to parasympathetic tone in the autonomic nervous system (ANS), and a blood-thinning effect. The research, along with many anecdotal reports, is presented in a new book entitled Earthing"[13]

Embodiment

All the practices mentioned so far can help you to be more embodied, which is to live with an awareness that extends throughout your body. Conscious embodiment is often an

---

[12] Gaétan Chevalier, Stephen T. Sinatra, James L. Oschman, Karol Sokal and Pawel Sokal. 2010. *"Earthing: Health Implications of Reconnecting the Human Body to the Earth's Surface Electrons."*: https://www.ncbi.nlm.nih.gov/pmc/articles/PMC3265077/#B12.

[13] Ober C, Sinatra ST, Zucker M. *"Earthing: The Most Important Health Discovery Ever?"* Laguna Beach, Calif, USA: Basic Health Publications; 2010

important part of healing. This is because many people live from their heads, and not from an embodied and whole place.

This is exhausting due to perhaps a bombardment of thoughts or because it means you will be less in touch with your body's changing needs. It also means you are living from a more contracted and small sense of yourself. It's important to slowly come home fully into this body, to actually fully inhabit our body with our awareness. Step 7 of healing your past will help you with this, as the more you do this, the easier it is to be fully present in your body.

Can you bring your awareness into the soles of your feet now, feel your fingertips, be aware of your pelvis… etc.? Be aware of the breath going in and out of the body. The more we are embodied and present here, the happier and healthier we will be.

Sometimes people use spirituality as a way of escaping being fully present here, and I confess that I was one of those people for a couple of years. My feeling now is that true wholeness and happiness comes from inhabiting our body fully. Indeed, that is it is the gateway to who we really are, to be in the awareness that fills our body, our essential aliveness, the capacity we have for full and conscious embodied awareness.

Oxytocin

Oxytocin is a natural stress releasing hormone, that is released through physical contact and emotional bonding. Regular hugs, massage and deep connection can help to release this 'feel good' and healing hormone into our body. As I mentioned, one of the organisations I work for, Women's Wellness Circle, is in part about bringing women together to nurture the connection, and the oxytocin that is released, when women come together in a conscious way. We also use conscious touch to support this.

You can support oxytocin to be released into your system right now by giving yourself a little massage or a hug. And women, I invite you to include your breasts and nipples in your massage, which are particularly powerful to release oxytocin.

Salt Baths

Salt baths are a great way to support detox, promote relaxation and replenish mineral stores in the body. Have them regularly as part of your self-care routine.

Receiving Bodywork

As an additional support to building resources for your healing I recommend you receive bodywork with a recommended practitioner: The Rosen Method, The Bowen Technique, Acupuncture, Cranial-Sacral Therapy and Massage are my personal favourites. You might want to explore different methods and find what works well for your body and where you are now in your healing.

Follow your Joy

As we move towards the end of this chapter I must mention the power of following your joy in life, and in your self-care. As well as the self-care practices described, it's essential we have time where we are focused and engaged in something we enjoy.

I remember as I healed, I got into making cards. This helped get me through a time of despair about everything and feeling fed up with being unwell. I would spend some time every day absorbed in making cards. I've had clients who have got into crochet, knitting, colouring books, playing a musical instrument and writing poetry.

To help you with this, explore doing it in bite-sized pieces, and do what you can. For instance, I have one client, Anna, who loves to garden and yet is not currently well enough for much gardening. Instead, she makes sure she does a 10-minute plant potting task most days or at least gets out into her garden for a short while.

Follow your joy with the self-care practices you adopt on a regular basis and in the way you approach The Lotus Process. Remember I mentioned earlier the client who had a big a-ha moment with realising how hard she was pushing to be well all the time and even in her so-called idea of 'self-care'? Letting go of pushing was a key to making a recovery. Follow your joy with self-compassion for where you are at this stage of your healing.

Creativity

As I started to touch on in the previous paragraph I must emphasise the power of allowing space for your own creativity to flow, however, it wants to flow through you. For some it's singing

Step 3: Self-Care and Inner Resources

in the shower, or expressing yourself through words in a journal, colouring, dancing or painting with your toddler. The bottom line is, creativity is a deeply natural force. It is a fundamental part of your being, and your health and happiness can depend on how much you are allowing it to flow through you.

Science proves that being creative builds new brain cells. It also helps you to keep balanced. Our brain is divided into the left and right hemispheres, the left being the side that takes care of logical, rational aspects of our lives, and the right side controlling the irrational, emotional and creative aspects.

We need both hemispheres to be activated and cultivated in order to be balanced healthy beings. We in the modern, Western world tend to be pretty good at the left brain stuff; organising, deadlines, plans and analysing. We can fob creative, right brain activity off as pointless or a waste of time because it doesn't produce anything.

Retreats and Holidays

To support you in building your resources, I highly recommend going on a retreat at least once a year and a holiday at least once a year too. Retreats give you a beautiful space away from daily life to embrace wellbeing tools that can last you a lifetime. They foster the opportunity to deeply drop into a space of greater peace and ease in your body-mind system. Retreats offer you space to connect with others and to deeply connect to your own core. They give your system space to start the process of healing your past. The picture below is a view near Nabb cottage in the Lakes where Sophie and I have held our last two Women's Wellness Circle retreats.

Holidays are clearly great for you, whether you go locally or travel further, to have space from your normal life, to perhaps explore nature, be on a beach or to spend time relaxing with friends or family. They all can be deeply enriching for you. I've had many clients comment that once they're on holiday, perhaps in the sun, symptoms have dropped away completely!

In this respect, do what you can with what you have, you can splurge on a luxury retreat or holiday experience, or there are Buddhist retreats you can go on that are run on 'dana' or generosity and you pay what you can afford. A holiday can be cheaper if you book early, go somewhere local and perhaps stay in an Airbnb venue. This summer my family and me had an amazing Airbnb holiday with another family; it was very reasonably priced, on a self-sustainable project in Herefordshire where we could pick our own fresh vegetables every day.

Self-Regulating your Nervous System and Rewiring your Brain

Much of what has been introduced here will help you to learn the power of self-regulating your own nervous system. This is essentially about being able to support the movement from an inner stress state to an inner state of healing.

This is also about rewiring your brain and creating new neural pathways that support you on your healing path and there are many ways to do this weaved through this eight-step process. As we follow these methods we are engaged in a process of rewiring the pre-frontal cortex part of the brain, at the front of the forehead.

The 'A Pause' exercise overleaf is another method to support you to self-regulate your nervous system and to rewire your brain. This is a process that you can do on a regular basis in a short amount of time. This will help you to help maintain the benefits received from meditation and everything that has been introduced so far.

~'A Pause' Exercise~

This exercise is to work with a pattern of thought that is holding you back in some way, for example:

- thoughts about symptoms or illness

- thoughts that relate to a personality trait that sabotages your recovery (Learn more in Step 5, Overcome Blocks and Personality Traits)

- when you have a decision to make and your mind is jumping back and forth

A ~ Awareness

P ~ Pause

A ~ Aaahhhhh

U ~ Understand

S ~ Support

E ~ Embody

1) Become **A**ware of a thought pattern, name it and describe how it feels in your body.

2) Say '**P**ause' out loud and bring one hand to your heart and one to your belly, to anchor the word and yourself in your body. Smile and feel your connection to the earth beneath you.

Step 3: Self-Care and Inner Resources

3) Stretch, yawn, shake and sigh; **A**aaahhhhh. Do whatever helps you to let go.

4) Now, take the stance of becoming your own **U**nderstanding and compassionate best friend. Put one hand on your forehead and one on your heart briefly, and change your position a little, perhaps by straightening your spine and allowing your chest area to open. You could imagine a lotus flower opening in your heart.

5) From the viewpoint of your best friend or mentor, what would you say to **S**upport the part of you that has the challenging thought pattern or feeling? Perhaps…

    'Relax, everything is going to be okay',

    'Keep going, you're doing really well',

    'You matter' or 'I love you'.

    'Other people have healed and you can too'

    You may want to offer yourself a hug.

6) Take a moment to **E**mbody and envisage a positive state which feels like the opposite of where you started. Find a positive, resourceful feeling: energised, calm, grounded, trusting… Here you can use a future visualisation of health, like I introduced in the last chapter, or a past positive memory, to help you to truly embody this state.

I suggest you also write the steps of 'A Pause' down on pieces of paper and step through the different positions. Essentially, six pieces of paper to represent:

1. Awareness

2. Pause

3. Aaahhhh

4. Understanding

5. Support

6. Embody.

I recommend you take yourself through the process in this way at least twice a day, and the other version as a shorter way of doing it several times a day. If your mind is very busy, it might be helpful to practice it 50-100 times a day initially to really support activating the healing response.

Stepping into different positions can help the process work at a deeper neurological level, as there is something powerful about this to access different states or parts of ourselves to create change in the brain.

To hear me guiding you through this process, visit my website www.lotusprocess.com to download The Lotus Process resources PDF with a link to a YouTube video.

Summary ~ Step 3: Build your Inner Resources

In this step, we have covered a lot. If you take one thing away, remember to look after yourself with compassion on a daily basis and follow your joy. I suggest you start with a morning meditation before breakfast, and use 'A Pause' as and when needed throughout the day.

You might just choose one exercise from this chapter to embrace fully for now and integrate into your life, and come back when you are feeling the need for some fresh resources to support your healing. You are so worth resourcing yourself well. In the next chapter, we'll start to explore the value of external support and resources in your healing.

Chapter 8
Step 4: Community and Support

"Jump to your feet, wave your fists,

Threaten and warn the whole universe

That your heart can no longer live

Without real love!"

~ Hafiz

There is so much you can do to build your inner resources and resilience, which we covered in the previous step. And, we are social animals and benefit greatly from having external support systems in place in order to thrive. This step covers the power of community, relationships and being surrounded by loving support, in order to enhance your healing path.

Friends, Family and Community

As well as daily living tasks, space to meditate, work (if we are currently working) and our exercise routine (however small at the moment), we need to have time in our diary each week devoted to quality time with our family, our friends and our community.

As social beings we need interaction with others to feel connected and happy. Isolation can quickly lead to depression, illness and decline, whereas having regular contact with others creates a sense of community and support, and helps us to thrive. We all benefit from having a sense of belonging to a tribe.

Options for supportive group spaces might be to find a local meditation or Buddhism group, a yoga class, starting a new course like art or a local women's or man's group. It could mean to reach out to friendship groups more regularly, or to create new ones. There are also online groups you can join. I run various online groups for women healing chronic illness so get in touch with me if this may be of interest.

I cherish my relationships with my family, my partner and my friends. I have had deep personal experience of their importance for my health and wellbeing. When I was recovering from Chronic Fatigue, it was the support and encouragement of my community that gave me the confidence I needed to heal.

If you are currently feeling very isolated and this chapter is bringing up a sense of loneliness for you, feel free to focus on the other steps more at first to build your inner resilience as well as making baby steps towards expanding your sense of connection with others. I invite you to come and find The Lotus Process Facebook group to reach out and connect with others that are using this book to support their health recovery.

An important aspect of the recovery journey is often to be able to ask for help, to develop the confidence to expand your social network and make contact with people. To be able to let love in, as well as give it out. I remember a friend of mine assertively telling me I needed to learn to ask for help and be open to receive it. She told me that it was actually a gift to her, that she longed to be able to help me. Having this kind of support around

Step 4: Community and Support

me, even when it was painful at times to be authentically challenged, was also helpful in realising some core patterns I had that I needed to change.

With this in mind I encourage clients to develop their close relationships, as huge resources while they heal and for the rest of their lives. If they don't currently have such support in their lives, to go out and find it. It's difficult of course depending on the severity of the illness, but a sense of isolation or loneliness will only make a condition harder to heal. Get what support and connection you can, even if it's primarily online initially.

It can be really helpful if you find your tribe and thereby be surrounded by people who get your mindset and the journey you are on. Those that validate you and help you to believe in yourself. We are highly influenced by those we surround ourselves with, so it's important to cultivate the friendships where there is a mutual exchange of giving and taking, and relationships that generally give you a sense of joy and happiness. Of course, things can come up in any relationship, but you want to surround yourself with as much positivity as possible.

It might be helpful to connect to meditation or yoga groups or to find online sanctuary's where you can connect to others on a similar journey. For instance, many women find our Women's Wellness Circle Facebook group a deeply supportive place and have commented about how much it has helped to have a sense of belonging with women on a similar journey. As I mentioned, there is also a Facebook group for those following The Lotus

Process to connect with others following these steps through this book or online, and to stay in contact with my resources and support systems.

I had a client, Rachel, who was able to go from a place of feeling isolated and alone, to realising how much love there was in her life, and how she could reach out for more of it. This love became a huge resource as she healed.

Do you eat with your family or friends as much as possible? Sharing breakfast, lunch and/or dinner is a great way to have a daily dose of connection and mutual support.

Do you make space in your diary for quality time with family or friends? The simple act of sharing a meal, going to the cinema, going on a night out, a countryside walk, a trip to a spa, attending a yoga class, a retreat or workshop together can create a deep connection.

Do you laugh with others often?

If the answer to any of the questions is 'no', take the time to prioritise your relationships as a key way to support you to heal, and then to maintain your health and wellbeing. For some of you, it may mean making steps to expand your social network, perhaps getting out to join a group, doing some voluntary work or anything that helps you meet people. Perhaps you could also consider getting in touch with an old friend or two.

Do you hug and touch those you are close to often? Physical contact releases stress reducing oxytocin. Look for ways to have physical nourishment in your life with those you are close to, and it will increase your health and happiness.

Laughter

It can be difficult to find anything to laugh about when you are feeling unwell, but laughter has an amazing physiological effect on the body. Laughter will encourage the nervous system to calm down and will thereby support your health recovery journey.

As you may know, there are now "Laughter Yoga Clubs" being set up around the world, where people get together simply to laugh! You could also watch Laughter Yoga on YouTube. In the same way, although you may not feel like it, laugh out loud as much as possible - the neurological effects are very powerful! Sometimes we have to give ourselves permission to be happy, to smile through adversity. Of course, you can also watch or listen to comedy to get some healing laughter into your life.

Laughter really is the best medicine! It raises our pain threshold, as well as having lots of positive effects on the immune system and your nervous system. Sometimes with physical symptoms, we may not feel like laughing, but I encourage you to break through that feeling and laugh as much as you can, as open and as heartily as you can.

Sexual Relationships and Tantra

Having a healthy sex life can really support a healing path, as the sexual energy is a powerful force within us that can be harnessed to support physical healing. I also get that illness can get in the way, due to lack of energy, health or inhibited libido. I recommend finding a way to keep in touch with your sexual self even when it might feel less available when you're unwell, to support you to heal.

Practices such as Tantra, use the sexual energy to be guided towards emotional and physical healing. You might consider reading a recommended book on Tantra or finding a good teacher[14]. You can do many of the practices alone or with a partner.

Many people have sexual issues due to an abusive experience or simply the society we live in distorting our body image and relationship with sex. Starting to tenderly address these issues (refer to Step 7 on Healing your Past) and to feel comfortable in your body and with healthy intimacy can be very healing.

Women's Circles

One of the foundations for the development of Women's Wellness Circle was to provide spaces for women to connect and support each other as they heal. Many women have commented, in our Facebook circle, for instance, that having a supporting space for women has been so healing. A place to feel connected.

On our retreat last year in the Lake District we had women moved to tears arriving into the sacred and safe space of the women's circle. Imagine a beautiful room, with soft music playing,

---

[14] I am aware this is a big topic to touch on, I recommend a book in the resources section at the back and a reputable teacher.

with women welcoming you to come and lie down in a circle, to be covered with blankets, candles lit and a wood burning stove making the room warm and cosy. A lovely view of nature and trees outside. Men, you can imagine this too, there are spaces out there that are designed for men as well and run by women. There are also men's groups that can be very supportive spaces for personal growth and healing.

Oxytocin and Women's Circles

As I mentioned before, Women's Wellness Circle is all about building a supportive tribe of women. The women in our community support each other on our live events, our online groups and in our Facebook group. For example, one woman in our tribe, who was currently housebound with severe physical symptoms, recently mentioned it was a life-line for her to have this community of support and connection.

Women's Wellness Circle is also about supporting the release of stress reducing oxytocin through the connection and belonging that is experienced when women gather together in a conscious way, also through one of our primary practices being a self-massage routine[15]. At our in-person events we include safe and gentle touch to support healing and to meet the physiological and psychological need for touch.

Interestingly, up until about twenty years ago all stress research was done on men. The female body's hormones fluctuate so

---

[15]This practice is influenced by the courses Sophie and I have done with The Awakening Women Institute founded by Chameli Ardagh

much that it is challenging to measure hormonal responses, so researchers didn't include them in their studies. Thankfully, a group of pioneering researchers realised the madness of this and embarked upon ground-breaking research. What they found could have a potentially radical impact, for women, especially women who are engaged in a healing journey of any kind.

Their studies show that the typical 'fight, flight or freeze' stress response isn't the whole story. As well as this typical response the female body also responds to stress with a flush of different hormones, including Oxytocin, which instead creates an attitude of 'tend and befriend'[16]. In times of stress, women don't just move to run or fight, they reach out to protect and connect. I believe this also happens to men but to a lesser degree.

Oxytocin is a natural de-stress hormone. It helps muscles to relax, reduces blood pressure and reduces cortisol levels. It increases pain thresholds, has anti-anxiety effects and it promotes healing[17]. Hugging a friend, cooking a meal for someone you love, petting your dog, even giving yourself a 30-second shoulder rub can release oxytocin and its host of healing effects. Oxytocin has also been called the 'Goddess' and 'hugging' hormone.

At Women's Wellness Circle we believe the oxytocin-inducing friendship and bonding within women's circles can have tangible, measurable healing effects for chronic health problems. That

---

[16] Psychology Today. 2016. *"Tend and Befriend"* quotes the term coined by Shelley Taylor: https://www.psychologytoday.com/articles/200009/tend-and-befriend

[17] Sahelian, R. MD. 2016. *"Oxytocin hormone natural ways to increase, benefits and side effects"*: http://www.raysahelian.com/oxytocin.html

Step 4: Community and Support

combining this circle of support with tried and tested therapeutic tools, we can accelerate a healing path.

In our oxytocin drenched online immersions and retreats, we also share the tools and practices that most supported our healing, including Restorative Yoga, Emotional Freedom Technique, Neuro-Linguistic Programming, and guided meditation, relaxation and feminine embodiment practices from the yogini tradition of the Awakening Women Institute. All of these practices are woven through this eight-step method. The picture on the next page is from the end of our latest retreat in the Lakes.

Therapeutic Support

As we move towards the end of this chapter I must highlight the value of working with a coach or practitioner who gets from the inside out the path of health recovery. Someone with whom you feel safe and whom you trust. Someone who can hold you accountable for your own self-care while supporting you and guiding you through some of the parts that might be difficult to work on alone, such as step 7 of healing your past. There are many wonderful practitioners to choose from, and if you feel drawn to work with me or someone I can recommend to you, you'll find out more information on this through visiting my website.

Energetic Support

I believe there is a field of healing and support that is out there, on an energetic level, and that can be a powerful resource to tap into as we physically heal. This could be the energy of a spiritual figure we connect to, or to nature and the life force that flows through all of life. Even the energy of this book and everything that's gone into writing it, all the different sources of support received from others and evolved in myself. This healing field can be tapped into as a resource for you as you make these steps. The exercise on the next page is a way to support you to open to a wider field of support.

This is one of those moments when I emphasise again to take what helps you and leave the rest. If it helps you to have a sense of the bigger mystery that is helping you as you heal, feel it; if it annoys you or simply doesn't resonate at this moment, let it go.

Step 4: Community and Support

~Field of Support Exercise~

Feel free to take 5 minutes, 20 minutes or as long as you like for this exercise.

Find a comfortable sitting or lying position.

Take a moment to become aware of your whole body.

Feel into a sense of gratitude for any support that is in your life, perhaps reflecting on any people who love and care about you in simple or big ways. If you don't have this in your life now, call on wider support as described below.

Tap into your sense of the wider support that is out there. Perhaps feeling a connection to nature, to an ancestor that you loved but is no longer here or if you are that way inclined to a spiritual figure you connect with, the energy field of this book or something that inspires you.

Open your heart to receive this support. To support yourself in doing this drop into your heart area and feel the spaciousness in your heart.

Close by giving yourself a hug.

Summary~ Step 4: Community and Support

In this step we have covered the value of a supportive community in the process of healing. You are so worth getting the external support and validation you deserve.

In the next chapter, we'll start to explore overcoming internal sabotage to health and healing. Having a good community around you will help you navigate this important territory on the next step of The Lotus Process journey.

Chapter 9
Step 5: Overcoming Blocks to Healing

"Your task is not to seek for Love, but merely to seek and find all the barriers within yourself that you have built up against it."

~ Rumi

In this step, we will be covering the kind of personality types that might have been a part of what led to you becoming unwell in the first place, and can hinder your recovery journey. In addition, we will be working on overcoming the roots of certain traits that are out of balance or unsustainable, whilst honouring and harnessing the positive qualities and gifts of your personality. This will support you to be in balance, even if you still have these tendencies as part of who you are. We will also be delving into other unconscious blocks to healing and how to overcome them.

Survival Strategies and Personality Tendencies

As human beings we often develop survival strategies during childhood that don't always serve us later in life. For instance, we might have become overly focused on external success as that's how we got approval in our family home, but this has been to the detriment of our physical health longer term. We might have been overly focused on helping others, because, for example, we had too much responsibility for a sibling or parent.

Often physical health difficulties can be a manifestation of a pattern of behaviour that has created stress on the whole system.

If one particular organ is affected, it might be an emotion that is not being dealt with that is being held in the organ creating disease within it.

Take a moment to go inside and see if you can relate to any of these tendencies within yourself:

1. Do you want to keep the peace with others to the detriment of yourself and your health?

2. Do you focus on helping others but not yourself?

3. Are you very focused on external achievement and success?

4. Do you criticise yourself a lot?

5. Are you aware of allowing yourself to feel (and let flow) the whole range of human emotion: happiness, joy, love, sadness, grief, anger, rage, fear…? Or do you suppress certain feelings?

6. Do you have tendencies to see yourself as a hopeless victim?

7. Do you have a need to control others or your environment in order to feel safe?

8. Do you have a sensitive nature and struggle to see it as a positive?

9. Do you get in an anxious loop?

If any of these questions stir awareness of these tendencies within yourself, bring compassion to these parts of yourself. Bring a kindness to these tendencies, knowing that they were created a long time ago, and were probably a survival strategy to get you through a difficult time. Reflect on how they how they are unsustainable and how you can develop them to support your healing. Below I give some possible antidotes to the above tendencies, perhaps you need to:

1. Deal with conflict in a more assertive way.

2. Learn to love and help yourself first.

3. Know your own inherent value as a human being.

4. Learn to be kinder towards yourself

5. Learn to feel the full spectrum of emotions and to be able to let them flow when they arise, as well as to find spaces to release and let any suppressed feelings flow safely.

6. To take more responsibility for yourself and your healing.

7. Cultivate a sense of internal safety by developing the wise and compassionate part of yourself.

8. Learn the importance of boundaries for you as a sensitive type, the gifts you have such as empathy and that you can still have an inner strength.

9. Learn to break the cycle of feeling anxious about feeling anxious, that perpetuates the issue. Perhaps the art of feeling the deeper feelings beneath surface anxiety and making room for these feelings to flow.

Towards the end of my recovery journey from ME/CFS in my early twenties, I realised that I had a tendency to want to keep the peace at all costs, even to my health. Recognising that pattern and starting to change it, I noticed a big shift in my energy and my health. At this time, I was living in a house that belonged to my mum and we were renting out a room to someone who we needed to move out. I kept delaying telling him because there was always a reason it wasn't the right time to mention it.

I was keeping this information inside because I was scared of upsetting him and losing the sense of peace that we had. I was not being honest to the detriment of my health and I realised I needed to fundamentally change my behaviour. Through this, I learned to be more honest and authentic with people, even if there might be conflict or it might be difficult for them to hear. This was a real key for me to be able to get well and stay well.

Learning about the Enneagram personality system (see the Appendix for more information) and that I was a 'nine' or a 'peacemaker' was really helpful around the time of noticing the pattern of avoiding conflicting. I realised I had an underlying pattern of 'keep the peace at all costs, even to my health'. I would avoid conflict. I would numb out to avoid difficult feelings and circumstances. You can probably see how these tendencies can put stress on the nervous system and be part of the puzzle that leads to chronic illness.

Sophie's story as a 'helper'

'I was running a yoga school and I managed to get burnt out as a yoga teacher. Which is quite ironic in itself because I was pushing myself too hard and there was a beautiful motivation behind my teaching, I really did want to serve people, but there was also a lot of helper style feelings of being a martyr. I surrendered my whole life to these people. And also people pleasing, wanting to impress my teachers, wanting my students to like me. So it was a fusion of both. So it was both good and bad intentions. So I pushed myself really hard. The helper personality was driving and pushing me until I crashed and I actually couldn't move for a week. And that was the start of my chronic digestive challenges journey.'

Sophie is my colleague at Women's Wellness Circle and has healed from severe digestive pain and nausea. Here's a recent picture of us.

The Highly Sensitive Person

Another important trait to consider is the highly sensitive person. People with this personality type seem to be more likely to develop chronic illness. There are great gifts to being highly sensitive such as being empathic. However, it can be difficult because you can feel the feelings of other people, and take on those emotions as your own. This can affect your own energy and health. You're also more likely to get tied into complex, difficult and energy-draining relationships.

Most of my clients, and I myself, identify with the highly sensitive personality type, and have found the book 'The Highly Sensitive Person'[18] a helpful resource. If you take it to mean you will never be able to heal, as you're just 'too sensitive' this can become an unhelpful identity. So hold it lightly, and know that you can be both sensitive and strong. I find my clients have often been told as a child 'you are too sensitive'; if this is you, I invite you to reframe your sensitivity as being okay and as a gift.

There is generally work to be done on building confidence and reassurance that you can be both sensitive and strong. Moreover, there are wonderful gifts of being sensitive such as deep empathy, and often being highly intuitive and able to read deeper meanings beneath the surface. There's just a need to develop resilience and strategies that help you to stay in balance. This might mean accepting that you need regular time alone or to be in nature on a

---

[18] Elaine N. Aron. 1999 *The Highly Sensitive Person: How to Survive and Thrive When the World Overwhelms You*. Thorsons

Step 5: Overcoming Blocks to Healing

daily basis. A client, Abigail, comes to mind, she realised that in order to recover and to stay healthy she needs regular time on her own in her garden, simply being.

Subconscious blocks

Subconscious blocks can take many forms. There can be parts of us that don't want us to be well, that feel we need to be ill to be protected or safe in some way. This could be, for instance, from a difficult relationship we are in or were in before the illness developed. It could be from a work environment we didn't like. It could be from past traumatic experiences, and it might even be inherited or modelled from parents.

I now understand that my illness was protecting me from a world that didn't seem fully safe. It didn't feel safe to be seen for who I was or to speak up. This is in part because of a physical attack as a teenager and other experiences in my personal life. I also later recognised it was from my ancestry. My Grandfather lost his parents in the Holocaust when he was a teenager. My belief is this led to a deep embedded sense of fear within me. I was only conscious of the link to my ancestors many years later when I started to explore the field of 'systemic constellations'[19]. The fear was lurking beneath the physical symptoms. In way my illness was protecting me from having to be in the world and deal with

---

[19] What has been termed 'family constellations', 'systemic constellations' and simply 'constellations' stems from the work of Psychotherapist Bert Hellinger. It is a way of working with a bigger or 'systemic' perspective on any issue, to support insight and resolution. The approach can be used in a group or one to one setting.

potential difficulties, which I now believe had its roots in my ancestry.

As a simple example of subconscious blocks to healing, one of my clients, Mathew, got unwell while in a job that involved bullying. The illness became a form of protection that allowed him not to be in such an environment, which then became a block to getting well. That is until he learnt to update his subconscious that he would not go back to that environment, and will be creating a new life once well.

Illness can also be a way of setting boundaries. For instance, if you are a helper, a chronic people pleaser all your life, illness can be a way of having a reason to say no because you do not have the energy to say yes to everything. I've had clients that are afraid of getting well because they feel they might need to start saying yes to everything again, so this can be a block to getting well until it becomes consciously transformed.

Trauma and Underlying Fears

Although we will talk more about healing trauma from the past in step 7, it is worth mentioning here as trauma can be beneath some of the personality traits, survival strategies and unconscious fears. Many of the clients I have worked with have experienced some kind of trauma in their lives, whether it's birth trauma, childhood trauma, bullying or difficult medical procedures, as examples. Perhaps a parent had a mental health problem or was an alcoholic.

In addition to this it is also important to note that trauma doesn't have to be an obvious big trauma. Indeed, it can be a buildup of smaller events, such as the way a teacher spoke in the classroom when you were seven and the effect this has on you. Anything that is unprocessed can be considered a trauma and might need to be released in order to reach a full and lasting recovery. Trauma often happens when you feel isolated and don't have a strategy for dealing with the experience.

Various life events have often led to this fear and a mistrust in the world. For many people, on an unconscious level, it can feel safer to be ill. Therefore, starting to address these underlying fears can be very helpful. Addressing the specific events or relational trauma that might support you to be happier in your own skin and to start to trust in life again, is a healing key for many.

Secondary Gains

Another aspect of chronic ill health to consider is that there can be secondary gains to being unwell. Two examples could be, the income of benefits or the attention of someone who cares for you.

Letting go of benefits can bring up survival fear, perhaps thoughts like 'will I ever be well enough to support myself financially?' or 'will I have to go back to a job that I hated'. Maybe when you're ill you get a certain level of support and attention that perhaps you didn't get before. I have worked with people that have an inner child that only got attention when ill, so as an adult this part of them can be recreating this pattern as a way to get the love they need.

Furthermore, when unwell, you may start to create a life where you are able to do more meditation, more yoga and thereby start to connect to a deeper sense of who you are. You're perhaps able to enjoy walks in nature, and time to read your favourite books. This can lead to a fear of going back into a stressful life, and losing this newfound peace.

I've met many people who recognise this pattern. Making a deep commitment to self-care even once you are well will help here. As will letting your unconscious know that it's not what you do, but how you do it. That even when life gets busier you will be bringing your new way of being into a fuller and richer life.

This all links into the personality types, for instance the helper might be afraid to go back to always helping others at a cost to their health. An achiever might be afraid of losing themselves in the pattern and causing health problems again.

The reality is that as you start to get better, you might go back into some of those roles. Growing your self-awareness of this and learning to moderate such behaviours can be crucial to sustaining your wellness. For instance, when I first got well there was a part of me that said I wasn't allowed to go on a retreat unless I was doing some form of work e.g. helping to cook on a retreat camp with 100 people. It took me a year to drop that idea, to stop pushing myself and just allow myself to enjoy a retreat for me.

Illness and Boundaries

Sometimes a block to healing can be that we feel we need the illness to protect us in some way, to create a boundary between us and other people or the world. For many, learning to put up boundaries is a key for a deep and lasting health recovery.

I have a friend and colleague, Paula, who suffers from Chronic Hypersomnia, which means she falls asleep pretty suddenly in the middle of the day. Through her growth and self-awareness, she has come to the realisation that falling asleep was a way of escaping difficult situations as a child which then became a learned behaviour in adulthood. Starting to bring compassion to herself was a key part of starting to heal; becoming the loving parent to herself, who can then make new choices. Choices that enable her to have more boundaries, including to say no when she needs to and therefore to stay awake in situations when she would've previously fallen asleep in.

Pacing

It's really important as you heal to build yourself up gradually. Tendencies like the 'doer' or 'achiever' can lead to a false sense of where you are and put you into stress. More stress generally means more symptoms will follow. It's important to sensibly increase physical or mental activities, and have restful pauses between activities or do practices like meditation. It's also important to have a balance of physical and mental engagements, actually things like being on the computer are more draining for the nervous system than taking a gentle walk outside.

I remember when I was recovering my health I read once that people with CFS often need to do more physically and less mentally. This seemed crazy on one level as at the time I was in such a weak physical state, but on another level I knew it was true for me. This encouraged me to start to go out for gentle walks, even when I felt really weak and like I was walking through treacle.

Once you're following all the steps of this process, it will be easier to know when you need to do more, and when it's time to do less. You'll be more aware of yourself and your current limitations, while remaining committed to the path of healing. You'll be calming you own system and building up your resources, so that you can gently start to do more in a paced way.

The Lotus Process Tools for Overcoming Blocks to Healing

In The Lotus Process the different tools you can use to support you in overcoming the various internal sabotages are EFT (Emotional Freedom Technique), Self-Compassion, NLP, The Wholeness Process and A Pause. These are all powerful tools that can support you to overcome internal sabotages to enable all parts of yourself to get alongside your healing efforts. On the next pages is a self-compassion exercise to explore, inspired by Buddhist loving kindness meditation and The Wholeness Process[20].

---

[20] The work of Connirae Andreas, find out more in the resources section at the back of the book and through accessing my recourses PDF at www.lotusprocess.com.

Step 5: Overcoming Blocks to Healing

~Self-Compassion Exercise~

Find a comfortable sitting or lying position

Take a moment to become aware of your whole body

Centre your awareness in your heart and see if you can get a sense of your heart opening towards yourself.

To help with this you may imagine a flower opening in your heart, a light coming out of your heart and filling your body, or saying words like 'May I be Well, May I be Happy, May I Heal, May I be Whole....' You could imagine these words like a pebble dropping into a lake in your heart and waves of self-compassion rippling out.

Be aware of where in your body you are experiencing tension or emotions, and gently hold these parts in a field of compassion

Be aware of any parts of you that might be holding back your recovery: Perhaps the achiever, helper or peacemaker. Perhaps a part of you that holds fear. Notice the location in the body and felt sense of this part of yourself e.g. is it hard, prickly, watery or smooth?

Have a sense of the awareness that fills your body and is around your body. Feel the field of compassion in your heart open and expand too. To help you to do this see if you can sense the spaciousness in your heart.

Invite a dissolving and melting of where you feel any physical sensations or emotion into the full field of awareness and compassion

Have a sense of the awareness that fills your body and is around your body too. This awareness is like your fundamental consciousness that can also sense the space around you. Feel the field of compassion in your heart open and expand too.

Summary ~ Step 4: Overcoming Blocks to Healing

I hope this chapter has helped you to get in touch with some of your personal inner blocks to recovery and a sense of how to tenderly work with this important step on your healing path.

Finding a purpose to be well can be crucial to support you to keep moving forwards on your healing path, to be pulled out of the blocks and drawn towards health, which is the next step of The Lotus Process.

Chapter 10
Step 6: Purpose and Authenticity

"What is it that you plan to do with your one,

wild and precious life?"

~ Mary Oliver

This step covers the power of finding a purpose to be well to support you in keeping focused and committed to your healing path. It often helps if it is a purpose that is bigger than yourself in some big or small way, as most of us have a longing to contribute to others of the world. In addition, it covers the importance of finding your own authentic purpose and learning how to show up as your authentic self. Indeed, this is how we will thrive.

Purpose

Finding a sense of purpose to be well can be a healing key for many on a health recovery journey. Most of us have a genuine need to feel we are contributing to others' happiness, or the world, in some way. It can be big or it can be seemingly small. There is an inspiration to heal that often goes beyond yourself as an individual.

Purpose is a healing key for many because it keeps you focused and committed to the path of healing. It gives you a sense of direction for where you are heading, and to keep going through the ups and the downs of the process. It almost pulls you along the healing journey to your desired future, the healthier you, doing what you love and are passionate about.

Your purpose could be to start a business you feel called towards, to work for a charity you feel moved to support, or maybe you really want to have a family and focus your time and energy on the important work of raising children well. Maybe you want to travel the world with your friend or partner and experience different cultures.

A client, Lucy, once said she didn't have any big ambitions or a sense of purpose. When we got to the topic of having the energy to grow her own vegetables and live more sustainably, she lit up in a way that was clear this could be a part of her bigger purpose in life. This helped to fuel the next stage of her recovery by providing a motivation to be well, something that could help to pull her along to this destination.

Ask yourself these questions to help get a sense of your purpose:

- What do you love?

- What inspires you?

- What are the wider causes you feel passionate about?

- Imagine being towards the end of your life, what do you want to have accomplished? Who do you want to have been?

It doesn't matter what it is, but having a sense of purpose can keep you on the path of the important task of following all the

Step 6: Purpose and Authenticity

steps that are needed for you to heal physically. To keep you focused on reaching your health goals, even when it doesn't make sense, even when you lose all hope. Having a purpose that helps you keep going no matter what. This purpose will be magnetic as it draws you to your future life, however large or humble it is.

For me my purpose became to get well and to help others to do so. At the time of my recovery journey there were fewer people that had recovered from CFS and related conditions, and less support available. Ultimately, I wanted to be a trailblazer of leading others to wellness too. Leaders in this field were emerging as I recovered and I soon supported their developments, before also establishing my own such as through Women's Wellness Circle and now with the development of The Lotus Process.

There was a time during my recovery journey where I felt really selfish because I was spending a lot of time doing inner work and meditation in order to heal. However, I had a realisation that I wasn't going to be able to help others, unless I healed myself first. With this in mind I developed a personal mantra, 'selfish so I can be selfless', to enable me to devote all this time to my healing. May your purpose, whatever it is, keep you inspired to keep going to make the inner shifts that are often required for a full and lasting physical healing.

In my work with people, I see that when they find a sense of purpose this helps them to stay committed to their journey back to health. It helps to pull them along the healing path to where they want to be. For instance, I have worked with younger clients who really wanted to start their own business in their personal passion, which has helped them to stay focused on all the steps to be well. In addition, I've worked with grandparents who long to be with their grandchildren more, and this has been a wonderful source of inspiration to keep going, and take all the steps to get there.

It's also important that you follow your authentic calling, not what you think you 'should' be doing or you feel society or your family expect of you. Be your authentic self, whether that means you want to work in a library, work with children, write books, travel the world or to become a healer.

On the next page is an exercise to help you to uncover what your authentic purpose could be.

~ Purpose Visualisation ~

Find a comfortable sitting posture. Start to let your mind float into your future well self. This could be you in six months, one year or two years.

What will you be doing with your life?

Who will be in it?

What does your inspiring and happy future look like?

What can you see?

How are you feeling?

What are you enjoying?

What are you able to do?

Spend 10 minutes imagining your best possible future. Really go into the experience as fully as you can, and enhance your sense of it by making it bigger, brighter and happier than you can possibly imagine. Do your best to make it what YOU really want (not your parents, not what you think society will approve of…)

Go even further ahead, imagine being towards the end of your rich and purposeful life.

What do you look back on and feel happy about?

What was really meaningful to you in your life?

After doing this exercise write down what you saw, and remember the power of creativity I talked about in step 3? You may like to create a vision board of your where you are going, perhaps cut out pictures, or draw, images that reflect the life you see in your future. You can put this on your wall as a reminder and to keep you motivated to keep going.

Being Your Authentic Self

It's essential as we heal to learn to honour our authentic selves, including: who we choose to be; how we express ourselves; the self-care that works for us; how we love and how we deal with conflict. As I mentioned above, it's important to follow your own authentic calling in life, not what others want for you or think you 'should' do. Should, ought, got to and must are words to take out of your vocabulary to help you to be kinder to yourself, happier and healthier.

The cost of not being authentically you is less health and happiness. When I was healing, learning to express my feelings was a key to recovering my health, even if it involved some conflict. In my work I've witnessed this pattern in many of my clients, who are so scared to show up authentically in their relationships, not wanting to upset anyone, wanting to keep the peace.

A client, Barbara, recently commented that an experience with a relative was transformed by using tools like EFT to help stop her getting emotionally tied into difficult communication. She was able to express herself assertively and actually be heard for the first time. I shared with her the 'cord cutting with EFT' exercise, a tool to help you untangle yourself from unhealthy relationship dynamics. There is a link to a video of this exercise in 'The Lotus Process' resources PDF you can download here: www.lotusprocess.com.

Summary ~ Step 5: Purpose and Authenticity

Living your unique purpose in life, and following it with authenticity, is key to moving towards the health you so deserve. Your purpose can be big, or small and simple, it just has to be meaningful to you. It often helps if it is contributing to others of the world in some way.

As well as following your unique purpose being authentic is also about how you express yourself and show up in all areas of your life. This, and all the other steps introduced so far, will enable you to embrace the next step, which for many is an important step on the road to full health and happiness. Starting to heal the past can help you to clear out of your nervous system and body anything else that might be blocking a full recovery.

Chapter 11
Step 7: Healing your Past

'In the broken places, the light shines through'

~ Leonard Cohen

Is our past our past? Have we truly left it there, or do we bring it with us in painful memories, thoughts, conditioned responses and body armouring? If we honestly ask ourselves that question many of us will find the answer is that we do indeed bring the past into our present life. This step will cover working with emotions, some science of what trauma is, how we heal and working with inherited trauma.

To be clear, we do not need to resolve all of our past baggage to heal physically, indeed we may not need to resolve any and the other steps presented here may be enough. However, I believe for a full and lasting recovery, it is helpful to gently explore the roots of our patterns and conditioning, and bring new resources to our younger parts. This will also support us in moving to a deeper place of peace and wholeness, and enriching our lives and relationships in amazing ways for the rest of our lives. As we heal our past we will develop more strength and resilience than we previously dreamed to be possible, and as we shall soon discover, we might even experience it as a spiritual awakening.

Healing your Past happens in the Present

Healing doesn't happen by getting lost in the feelings of the past. It is enabled by bringing new resources from the present to our frozen, fearful and sad parts in the present, and allowing release and relief to be brought into the nervous system. To be the most effective with this I suggest you work with a practitioner that you trust, and with whom you feel safe. For most people, this will be the most safe and effective way of integrating these parts and moving towards wholeness.

Some people resist the idea of 'healing the past' and think it is perhaps going over past hurts in a way that is not helpful. My approach is about gently touching what is there, and bringing wisdom and compassion from your adult self, to start to heal. Healing doesn't come through denial of the past, but neither does it come from wallowing in difficult feelings. It's a tender balance of touching with present moment awareness and freeing up your system from what it is holding.

Emotions and Health

Trauma and suppressed emotions can be part of the picture of what later manifests as a chronic health condition. For example, as I was healing from CFS and was in the final year of the illness and generally doing pretty well, I went to see my father by the coast. Within a day of being there, I ended up feeling really unwell and barely able to get out of bed for days. As I was laying there in despair about how ill I felt I suddenly had a feeling that my body was calling to me through these horrible symptoms to be really authentic with my Dad for the first time; to talk about how painful it was when I was a child and he split up with my mum, and what had led up it. Thankfully, he had recently been in therapy himself and so he was open to talking to me about it.

Once I realised this was what I needed to do I had the energy to go out for a little walk with him and from the start I brought up the topic. Telling me more about his story as we sat on cliffs looking out over the sea, we both ended up crying and connecting, and it was a beautiful and healing experience. It was also a moment of reinforcing the link between mind and body, as I felt so much better physically once I'd spoken my truth and been heard. I left feeling so much healthier and happier, and like a layer of what was needed in order for me to recover had been resolved.

Needless to say, it's not always possible to have these conversations with the people in your life that might have had a big impact on you. In which case therapeutic support can be really helpful and necessary to work through these feelings. Of course, if you've got really good friends that you can be truly authentic with, that can be very supportive as well.

Go Gently

Starting to touch into the themes of this step may bring up feelings for you now, I invite you to be very gentle with yourself and keep yourself safe. If feelings are being brought up I suggest you take a look around the room and orient yourself to the present moment, knowing that you are safe here and now.

Remind yourself of your name, present age and the date. Look at something that is comforting to you and give yourself a hug.

You might want to reach out to a friend or a family member whom you feel safe to share with, or a practitioner you've worked with before, or be in touch with me to find out what additional support systems I have available at the moment. If you have spiritual beliefs, you can lean into a sense of support from a figure that represents love and compassion to you and can help to hold you as you navigate this territory.

Working with a Practitioner

Once you've developed a strong inner container you might find you can also start to do deeper inner work on your own. However, I would suggest doing this as an addition to having outer containers of support. This could be in a one to one or group setting, with a practitioner that you feel safe with.

I say this as someone who is committed to a life-long path of growth and still has this support myself! Of course, I'm not suggesting you will always need or want it yourself. Although I do believe if you feel moved to become a wellbeing coach or therapeutic practitioner of some kind that keeping up your own personal growth, and getting support with this, is vital in being an ethical and continually evolving practitioner who can offer the best to clients. While you are in the process of healing, it can be fundamental to have this type of support for a full and lasting health recovery.

Inner Child

Working with your 'inner child' can be a powerful way to address healing your past, and thereby supporting physical health recovery. The 'inner child' can be thought of as parts of you that split off when you were young and come out in your present life. An indication that an inner child part might be present is if we are over-reacting to a situation. For example, I know I have an inner child showing up if I get really angry at my partner for something quite small. I'm transferring onto him some aspect of my unresolved past.

The inner child parts of us need some love and attention, essentially they need to be mothered in some way, in order to lessen their reactions. They might also want to experience being carefree and doing some simple activities that bring joy. Maybe your inner child wants to dance, to sing, to make daisy chains, climb trees or walk around the garden barefoot. You can ask her or him :-)

Attachment

Often many of us with chronic illness have not had the ideal secure attachment with our mother and/or father, that we really desired and our being innately expected. We come into this world expecting on a biological level that we're going to have a secure and safe environment.

Our parents always did the best they could with the resources they had and some more limited than others. Indeed, particularly in our modern societies, it is nearly impossible to bring up a child without there being some mark left on the personality or soul of the child. This is not about being perfect parents!

Your needs simply have to be met enough of the time to develop a secure attachment. If you don't get enough of the security you need, you adapt to cope. You develop an anxious, avoidant or ambivalent attachment style, with repercussions on your health, relationships and your life in general, until you start to address this and move towards a secure attachment. Studies have shown that the insecure attachment styles can be linked to chronic illness, such as this study on the link between chronic pain and an insecure attachment style[21].

Developmental and Relational Trauma

The topic of attachment style also relates to trauma that is relational, such as the ongoing stress of a relationship, perhaps with a parent that is an alcoholic or has a mental health problem, and are therefore very likely to lead to a less secure attachment style. These kind of situations are also likely to lead to a 'parentified child'; a child that has held too much responsibility, affecting their natural development and carries this over-responsibility into their adult life.

Trauma can also be developmental, such as being told off for being naughty when having big feelings as a toddler, when it's

---

[21] K.A. Davies, a G.J. Macfarlane, b J. McBeth, R. Morriss, c and C. Dickensd. 2004. *Insecure attachment style is associated with chronic widespread pain*: https://www.ncbi.nlm.nih.gov/pmc/articles/PMC2806947/

natural to need adults to help you regulate your feelings, or being overly responsible as a child for a parent or sibling. The natural process of your development will not have been able to complete, so you might need to allow yourself to have some tantrums (in the right setting!) or to experience being a carefree child, to help compensate for this.

EFT and PTSD

EFT and Meditation are approaches in The Lotus Process that are now getting recognised as a viable treatment for PTSD. A recent article in a prestigious psychiatric journal reviews pharmacotherapy, psychotherapy and 'non-pharmacological somatic therapies' as treatments for PTSD. It refers to EFT (along with acupuncture, mindfulness and yoga) as 'emerging methods for treating PTSD with moderate-strength evidence'[22]

Trauma: Unexpected, Dramatic, Isolated, No Strategy

UDIN is an acronym taught in EFT training to describe what trauma entails[23]. That it is Unexpected, Dramatic, we are Isolated and we didn't have a Strategy. You can understand, I'm guessing, that something that is unexpected and dramatic could prove to be traumatic, as can the experience of isolation alongside this. Often

---

[22] Nils C. Westfall, MD; Charles B. Nemerofff, MD, PhD. Psychiatric Annals. Sept 2016. "*State-of-the-Art Prevention and Treatment of PTSD: Pharmacotherapy, Psychotherapy, and Nonpharmacological Somatic Therapies*":
http://www.healio.com/psychiatry/journals/psycann/2016-9-46-9/{906528a9-bb05-4c5b-a9d0-d965dfb44e8e}/state-of-the-art-prevention-and-treatment-of-ptsd-pharmacotherapy-psychotherapy-and-nonpharmacological-somatic-therapies

[23] UDIN is an acronym coined by Flook R. 2013 *Why Am I Sick*. Hay House.

if after a traumatic situation we get the connection we need, the impact of the event will leave our system. In fact, this is the first place the nervous system wants to go to resolve a trauma, to 'friend'. Furthermore, it is also more likely to be traumatising if you do not have a strategy to resolve a situation. Indeed, there is evidence which shows if a person is in a traumatic situation and they try to escape or find a way out of the situation, they fare a lot better than those who numb out and don't do anything.

When we have a strategy, it enables us to complete some of the biological processes in the nervous system, rather than getting stuck. Many of you will have heard about the fight or flight response, which is how we respond to what we perceive to be a danger. It's also worth bearing in mind that what we perceive to be a danger might not actually be a danger. Events in your past that might not seem traumatic to your adult self, may have been experienced as traumatic for your child self at that particular time in his or her development. It has been suggested by someone with experience of working with a whole range of conditions, including heart disease and cancer, that UDIN needs to be present for disease to arise, that:

"when people go through a shocking experience that they are unable to deal with, it causes the body to change, freeze, fight, or defend itself. The criteria of the shock must be as follows: Unexpected, Dramatic, Isolating, and No Strategy. All of the criteria, which I call UDIN for easy reference, must be present for a disease to occur"[24].

---

[24] Flook R. 2013. P54-55. *Why Am I Sick*. Hay House.

Step 7: Healing your Past

Friend, Fight, Flight, Freeze and Flop

The fight or flight mechanism in the nervous system will calm down once a sense of safety is restored. However, if we experience trauma and we weren't able to fight or we weren't able to run away, we go down to the next strategy, which would be to freeze. When we freeze our whole system collapses and plays dead, and actually there's a deeper level of collapse that we can move to next, which is to flop.

As I mentioned earlier, the first response when there is a threat is to 'friend'. If this doesn't work then the system moves into the fight, flight, freeze or flop[25]. If we go all the way to freeze or flop and haven't managed to release it from our system, which often human beings and animals in captivity don't, it gets stuck. This can cause emotional, mental and physical health problems.

When animals in the wild experience a trauma they release the effect of the event with no imprint on their system. For example, if an antelope is nearly killed by a tiger, it will play dead. Afterwards, when the tiger goes off to get the lion cub to feed on this antelope, it can escape. It plays dead as a survival mechanism. Once the antelope is in a safe place again its whole system will start shaking, which will fully release the biological response from the experience. You can see examples of this on YouTube[26].

---

[25] A wonderful article on trauma that explores this and other related themes. Zoe Lodrick. 2010 *"Psychological Trauma – What Every Trauma Worker Should Know"*: http://www.zoelodrick.co.uk/training/article-1

[26] An example of this is at https://www.youtube.com/watch?v=eT4060GeodI

The animal will then continue as if nothing has happened to them. They've had a life-threatening experience, but it hasn't left any mark on their system afterwards. As we start to heal from trauma, our bodies might need to move, to shake or the body might need to say kick away what it wasn't able to do at the time of the initial trauma. The nervous system needs to complete what remains incomplete. There are ways of regulating this process so that it is safe and manageable for the system to move to a place of completion. This may take time. For me, this started to happen spontaneously as I healed.

Approaches like Somatic Experiencing and TRE can support this process of physical release through the body. This has happened naturally with many clients I work with, and I can incorporate this movement of the body into an EFT session or whatever approach we are working with at the time. For example, I remember a client telling me she felt like she needed to run, I asked her to imagine running or to gently make running movements, and after this, she felt her system calm down. Another client I worked with felt an urge to put her hands out to protect herself from a trauma of the past. I encouraged her to allow this to happen, gently and slowly, after some time her arms moved into a more flowing movement. I have another client whose head shakes as she releases deep holding patterns.

Recently I witnessed the natural process of trauma release. I was at a friend's house and her little girl fell down the stairs. My friend was there right away to hold her and soothe her tears and after some time the little girl started to shake. This is a good example of a traumatic experience, that through the connection and holding with her mum, she was able to release the memory out of the system in a few minutes. I very much doubt anything remains in her system from this event, however, had she not had this connection, had she not been able to shake and release, it could have left some shock and frozen energy in her system.

To really complete and release trauma the body memory needs to be included. In psychological terms, this is called the implicit memory, rather than the explicit memory which is the conscious memory of what happened[27]. This is one of the reasons why I focus on working with the body so much in my resources, sessions and groups.

I hope this explanation gives you an understanding that may support you as you heal. Body movements and shaking can be a system trying to discharge the energy, that is normal and actually a good sign you are in the process of healing. When I was meditating or when I was trying to do anything therapeutic, my system would start moving, shaking and wanting to complete actions. Learning about trauma really helped me to accept that process and see it as a normal part of healing.

Big T and Small t traumas

There can be big T traumas in life and small t traumas, the big T traumas may be abuse or a serious physical attack, a smaller t

---

[27] The understanding of explicit and implicit memory was solidified from reading Levine, P. 2015. *Trauma and Memory, Brain and Body in a Search for the Living Past, A Practical Guide for Understanding and Working with Traumatic Memory*

trauma might be the way a teacher spoke to you in the classroom or a mild bullying incident. The smaller events can still have an impact, though, it's good to be open to the fact that the little events can be experienced in a big way to your younger self.

I have worked with hundreds of clients over the past ten years and particular themes have emerged, such as experiences of bullying often at school or in the work place. Sometimes there has been abuse of some kind or living with a family member with an addiction or mental health issue. Starting to gently address some of these events and experiences can be really helpful to recover your health.

Healing Trauma as an Awakening

As we heal from trauma it can be experienced like a spiritual awakening, and we can develop levels of inner strength and resilience that we didn't have before. Peter Levine writes in one of his books[28]:

"Trauma represents a profound compression of "survival" energy…these same energies…can also open to feelings of heightened focus, ecstasy and bliss…it appears that the very brain structures central to resolution of trauma are also pivotal in various mystical and spiritual states."

Ancestral and Collective Healing

In recent years it has been discovered how we can hold the emotional pain of our ancestors, as well as the pain of the

---

[28] Levine, P. 2010 *An Unspoken Voice: How the Body Releases Trauma and Restores Goodness.* North Atlantic Books

collective unconscious, within our own bodies. As we continue the work of personal growth and healing this is the territory we may begin to find ourselves. It might be really helpful to explore this to get to the roots of your health issues and to support physical healing.

It makes sense that if there is unresolved stress in a previous generation, the results of this can ripple down to subsequent generations in terms of behaviour patterns and beliefs. It is not only this way that it can pass down in a family, but also through actual epigenetic changes to the genes. Thankfully though, our genes can be changed by healing work we do now:

"one of the studies that we published, maybe a year ago, showed that some epigenetic changes occur in response to psychotherapy. If we're saying that environmental circumstances can create one kind of change, a different environmental circumstance creates another kind of change." [29]

Personally, I recovered from CFS/ME by focusing on my particular life issues. However, in the years since recovery, I have followed the threads of tight places in my body that open up ancestral and collective issues that I have held within. This may not be necessary for everyone but it might be something to explore to support you on your health recovery path. This can be especially true if you've already done the previous steps pretty thoroughly, done a lot of work on your own personal history and yet are still not getting the health improvements you long for.

---

[29] Rachel Yahuda being interviewed by Krista Tippett. On Being. 2015.
http://www.onbeing.org/program/rachel-yehuda-how-trauma-and-resilience-cross-generations/transcript/7791

Moreover, this will support you to grow in happiness and wholeness too.

A recent book I have read[30] is all about using Systemic Constellations to support the resolution of illness. It explores many cases of illnesses resolving through the method, such as MS, type 2 diabetes, auto-immune illnesses, anaemia, psychogenic voice loss and Crohn's disease.

Themes like an unresolved issue with one's mother, a previous love relationship of a parent, war experiences, crime in the family and unresolved deaths in the family, can all be revealed to be a part of the picture of what leads to a chronic illness. The person with the illness may be connected to the unresolved issue or person (or people) involved, which is in the wider family system and affects the individual's health due to the stress that puts on their body. That is until they can learn to recognise what is there, open their hearts and disentangle themselves from it.

I have had clients who have done a lot of personal healing, and exploring ancestral issues provided a deepening of the healing process towards resolution. The ancestral level adds another dimension and level of understanding and has helped with the physical healing. We had many women at our recent retreat in the Lake District who found systemic constellations a powerful way to get beneath some of the core issues underlying chronic physical symptoms, to support moving towards healing. After doing such

---

[30] Hausner S (2011) *Even if it cost me my Life: Systematic Constellations and Serious Illness.* Gestalt Press

deep work many of their eyes and faces were lit up and one woman commented on the retreat that she had walked further than she had in three years! Another that she felt there has been a profound move forwards in her health since the retreat.

I believe my family history is what predisposed me to become ill. As I mentioned previously, I have Holocaust victims in my family so that's quite a big ancestral trauma, and research has shown that Holocaust survivors' relatives can be more predisposed to trauma and stress themselves. Hence it would follow to chronic illness and mental health problems too. That is until they start building an inner and outer environment that supports healing, and following a method like The Lotus Process.

While it's something I didn't look at specifically while I was unwell, it is something I have looked at since and I now see the wider perspective as to why I got so unwell when I was young. I'm not saying you need to be thinking about all these different levels at this stage, but just to open the door to a bigger perspective. The process of starting to heal this doesn't need to be traumatic, it can be simply about seeing what's been unseen or not dealt with in a family and also handing back with love what is not yours to carry anymore.

It is helpful to be aware of deeper conditioning from our family of origin; we are intrinsically linked to the whole family system. The two world wars had a massive impact on many of our grandparents and our parents, and on us in less obvious ways. Anything unresolved can filter down to future generations, unless someone opens their heart to it all, while letting go of the burden that is not theirs to carry, and releases the patterns and tendencies that have developed from these past experiences.

Forgiveness

A crucial aspect in healing our past is the power of forgiveness. Forgiveness is a choice we can make in order to give us peace and freedom. It is not about condoning what was done or who did it, but accepting and forgiving so we can be happy and move on with our lives. Holding onto resentments and hurts causes us stress, and stress leads to illness. In order to access the healing power of forgiveness, it is often necessary to move through layers of anger and sadness, and it may be necessary to have support with this from a therapist.

Forgiveness for the person or group of people is not something to be jumped to at a surface level, before any pain with the associated issue has been met and released. If there are deep wounds and traumas from the past, emotions associated with the memories need to be released too, before a true forgiveness and letting go can arise. Sometimes to get to this place you may need to feel anger and grief about past events, and maybe even express this to those involved, in order to get to a deeper place of forgiveness.

I think of a recent client, Sarah, who was able to contact the perpetrator of abuse from her childhood, and the remorse he expressed supported her in letting go of the incidents more deeply. This was a very brave act that deeply supported her forgiveness and healing process. I'm not suggesting doing this is always helpful, necessary or even possible, but it shows the power that can be found by actually confronting the people involved.

Self-forgiveness and self-compassion are also essential ingredients. If we've done anything we regret, remorse can be helpful for a period to support us in growing and evolving, however, we must learn to move onto a place of self-kindness and compassion. Many of us carry shame at a deeper level, which is exhausting for our bodies. The more we can find deep peace with ourselves, the quicker we will heal. Something that helped me as I healed was reading a booklet called 'The Final Surrender' about one woman's journey of healing ME. The final surrender to full and lasting healing was to move to a place of self-love and self-acceptance.

Starting the process of healing my past, and forgiving others and myself, was key to my ultimate full recovery from Chronic Fatigue/CFS. It amazes me how free my body is compared to how it was in the past. I used to find my shoulders up near my ears they were so tense, and I had a continual sense of anxiety and doubt in my solar plexus and diaphragm area.

Now, thanks to tools such as EFT and following the steps of The Lotus Process, I experience such a sense of lightness and freedom in my body. This only grows as I continue to use tools to release at deeper levels, being taken into the pain of my ancestors and the collective unconscious pain of the feminine. Allowing this to come through for healing, so that I can continue to grow in strength, love and freedom. May you experience the power and relief of this too, as you read this book and perhaps take the next step with this Lotus Process journey if you feel called to do so.

This practice encourages a deep trust in your body; one that many of us with chronic health conditions may have lost touch with. This trust in your own body wisdom is a deep home-coming to yourself and can be an ever-present source of grounding, confidence and possibility.

You Don't Have to Heal Everything!

I'm definitely not saying that you have to clear all the trauma from your life, or even touch on ancestral issues, to be well. This can continue afterwards if you wish to keep going with the work. You just need to discharge enough of what your system is holding in order to be physically well, and for that directly addressing the past might not be needed at all. It was a big part of my path, and it is of many of the clients that choose to work with me, so I talk about it a lot. However, I know of many people who have healed from illnesses like CFS without specifically addressing their past.

Grieving the Loss

The experience of becoming unwell, the realisation that illness won't disappear overnight, the persistence of the illness and all the symptoms, the mysterious and unfathomable nature of being unwell; all of these aspects of illness are a trauma too. These aspects can be something important to get relief around, especially the memories of the early stages of the illness and the impact it has had on your life.

Part of the process of full healing, I believe, is also to grieve what was lost at the time when you became unwell and during the years of illness. This can be another layer of the healing and coming to greater health and wholeness. This often starts to happen once you've made real headway with your healing journey. There is then the space to process the loss of those years of your life as an ill person. Even though you might have also gained a lot during those years; there is still a loss to grieve of what you couldn't do because of the illness and how much suffering there was during it.

Layers of Healing

There can be many layers that you may need to go through to support a full, lasting and sustainable health recovery. There might be one or two core issues that once you get to will lead to a resolution of your health problem. It is essential you take it one step at a time and move at a pace that our systems feel safe with.

The Lotus Process Tools for Healing the Past

In The Lotus Process, the different tools we currently use to support healing from chronic illness and healing trauma are EFT (Emotional Freedom Technique), Meditation, NLP, Wholeness Process, Bodywork and Family and Structural Constellations. These are all powerful tools that can support the healing and integration of traumatic memories and emotions held in the body.

The most appropriate tool will depend on where you are in your healing journey.

If you are generally healthy, learning and practicing tools such as EFT, will help you to maintain well-being and will also increase your sense of peace and happiness. If you are suffering from chronic physical and/or mental health challenges, these tools can become vital to restoring your health and wellbeing.

I know of a colleague who utilised EFT to work through traumas leading up to psoriasis. After only four sessions she was completely healed[31]. Here is one story of healing with EFT and there are countless examples of EFT helping people to heal from a whole range of physical health issues.

There are many practices that can help you as you contact emotions and traumas from your past, to provide release. I highly recommend starting this work with a practitioner or in a group setting that feels safe to you. Other tools and therapies for releasing traumatic memories and emotions from the body that you may like to explore are Trauma Releasing Exercises (TRE), Body Oriented Psychotherapy, EMDR and The Rosen Method. Of course, find out more about how I might be able to help you or point you in the direction of good support at my website. Next you will find a couple of exercises to start to support you with healing small t trauma and releasing emotions. I suggest you choose one of these exercises to practice now, and the other to practice at another time.

---

[31] Dr Annette Vaillancourt PhD, A Miracle in Slow Motion: How One Woman Healed Psoriasis with EFT in 6 Weeks

Step 7: Healing your Past

~ Expressing Emotions Through the Body ~

Recall a recent time you felt a strong, challenging emotion

Find the feeling in your body... If it is anger, perhaps you feel a tension in your jaw. If it is sadness, maybe a sinking in your chest. If it is fear perhaps you sense a tightness in your belly. Trust what comes.

Ask your body what it needs. Often anger wants to stamp, sadness wants to curl into a ball and fear might want to shake. Again, trust your first instinct.

For a couple of minutes, let your body do this action fully.

Now, place one hand on your belly, and one on your chest - and notice - what is present now?

~ EFT Exercise: Tell the Story Technique ~

This is a technique to work with a difficult memory. Choose a memory that is not too traumatic, is a small-t and just one event. Save the bigger and more complex memories for working with a practitioner.

Choose a name for the story, e.g. 'shouted at by Fred'. Give the memory a rating out of 10 (10 being it intensely affects you when you think about the title, 0 not at all)

Tap the side of the hand point 'Even though I have this......memory, I accept myself anyway' three times. Or 'Even though I have this......memory, and I feel......about it, I accept myself anyway'

Tap around all the points for several rounds on the name until the intensity comes down sufficiently to tell the story without excessive emotion, suggested to be less than a 4/10. You could also repeat the feelings the name of the memory stirs in you as you tap around.

Slowly start to tell the story of the event starting at the beginning before the intense event.

Stop as soon as any emotional disturbance is detected and tap on the last statement you made.

Test by re-telling the story from before the emotional disturbance. You should now be able to go past the previous sticking point easily. If not, there are further aspects remaining. Ask what is it about that that gives you that feeling? Tap further and only proceed with the story when this aspect is cleared.

When you feel calm on each aspect, continue the story. Stop to treat each emotional disturbance as it arises.

At the end test the title, and tell the entire story from the start to finish. You know you are complete when you can remain calm, at 0-1 intensity, with the title and throughout the story.

See the appendix for more information on the EFT process.

Summary ~ Step 7: Healing the Past

I hope you have a sense of the process of healing emotional wounds and trauma from your body-mind system. The potential power of this process to support a deep and lasting health recovery and to support you to move into a place of greater strength and resilience. Go gently and tenderly with this.

The next step is a vital step of learning to sustain your health, which will help you to stay in balance and keep the health benefits you receive as you recover your health.

Chapter 12
Step 8: Sustaining your Health and Wholeness

"May you keep faith with your body,

learning to see it as a holy sanctuary

which can bring this night wound

gradually towards the healing and freedom of dawn."

~ John O'Donohue

In this step we'll start by exploring the importance of learning to sustain your health once you get it. Secondly, how it's crucial to not get overly excited when you have a lift in physical symptoms. Thirdly, we'll look into how important it is to be aware of patterns that can re-surface as your energy and health come back, such as over-giving or over-doing. Fourthly, we'll explore setting up a life with ongoing self-care and following your joy. Finally, we'll also explore the possibility of keeping up with the journey of coming to deeper levels of spiritual wholeness after you are physically well.

Sustaining Health

From my own experience and working with hundreds of clients on their path to full health I know that this step is vital. I've seen people recover fully from a condition, and heal themselves through natural methods of say CFS or IBS, and then end up getting unwell again due to going back to old habits and forgetting the importance of ongoing self-care. I know someone who had cancer and recovered her health, and a few years later got Fibromyalgia, which she in part attributes to not learning the importance of self-care to sustain health.

It's also important not to go into to self-blame if this is you. We're always doing the best with the resources and understanding we have at the time. With hindsight, we might see our pattern. However, this is not a reason to beat yourself up, but to kindly commit to a new lifestyle and tend gently to the underlying issues.

Staying Calm and Centred

Once you recover, or at least start having windows of more health and energy, it can be important to stay calm and relaxed. One thing that happened to me as I recovered from CFS, and it's something I've witnessed in many clients, is an over-excitement about being well. An excitement that then overstimulates what is not yet a strong nervous system and can fuel symptoms to come back again.

Furthermore, the recovery process is an up and down journey for most people. If you stay calm and centred when you are feeling better, you are much more likely to be more relaxed about it if you do have a dip in health again. Enabling you to drop deeper into the first step of acceptance and surrender, which will support you in regaining your health again more swiftly.

Being Aware of Self-Sabotage

It's also important to not dive back into old habits, be it people pleasing, perfectionism or over-achieving. These patterns can all create stress in the system, again resulting in symptoms. If these patterns do arise, pause and notice, and make a new choice. You might want to book a series of sessions with a practitioner to help you unlock the root cause of the pattern and to support creating deep neurological change around this issue. Review Step 4 of The Lotus Process: Overcoming Blocks to Healing, as you make strides forward in your health. This will help to ensure old patterns aren't going to come back to sabotage your recovery, and to make a new choice moving forwards from now.

Ongoing Self Care

Self-care needs to become an ongoing thread in your life. That might mean to keep up a daily meditation or yoga practice, to learn something new like Chi Kung, or perhaps to spend some time in nature every day. It could mean having a close circle of friends that you see regularly or to have a regular date night with your partner. My recommendation is that you set up a life with support systems in place that meet you on a variety of levels, and fulfil a variety of needs.

Following Cycles

For menstruating women, I also recommend that you learn about the benefits of following the natural monthly cycle in the way you plan your month. Making sure you get some deep rest when you are on your period, especially on the first day. This is something my colleague and I have been teaching about at Women's Wellness Circle, and we feel this is an important approach to life that will help you stay well and benefit you for the rest of your life emotionally and physically. Menstruation is an opportunity for a deep resetting of all the systems of your body: by truly embracing this time you can experience renewed energy, vision and clarity.

For women who are not menstruating or for men, simply honour that there will be a natural flow of having more outward energy at certain times, and more inward energy at other times. Some women (and men I've heard too) have found following the moon cycle to be helpful in healing and sustaining health.

Following nature's seasons can also be deeply supportive. Simply put, with summer as a time for a full expressive life, slowing down for autumn, deeper rest in winter and tenderly sprouting new visions in spring is a great way to help your body-mind be in balance.

In order to support you to maintain your healing and wellbeing, it can be key to honour your natural inner rhythms and nature's outer cycles. Allow yourself times of rest when needed, you are so worth it.

Dealing with Symptom Flare-Ups

If you are generally doing well, and then go into a health dip or flare up of symptoms, it's important not to panic about it. Go back and touch what you learnt in step 1 about acceptance and surrender, in step 2 about belief and commitment and in step 3 about self-care and resources. This will help you to get back on track with your healing again.

You might like to gently inquire into what's happened: Have you gone back into old patterns? Has a present situation triggered off some past hurts to deal with? Do you need more balance in your life again? Trust that this is very transitory, and will shift and change soon the more you let go and relax.

Be kind to yourself no matter what. Be aware of patterns of obsessing about 'doing too much' or giving yourself a hard time. You'll get relief soon, and likely sooner than you realise is possible, especially if you are able to let go and trust.

Wholeness

In order to live a life of sustained health and wholeness, it is best if we continue the personal growth which was started as we have healed. Partly that's about finding the part of you that is whole, the part of you that is beyond all emotion, trauma, thoughts and memories of illness. We might think we're broken or deeply damaged, but for all of us, there is the potential to access and experience our unbroken and whole self. From this place we can be aware, present and embodied; and live a life that is deeply fulfilling.

The more we can access this inner source of wisdom, which can also be a compassionate inner holding, we can gently continue to move to deeper levels of wholeness. This can support parts of ourselves that feel separate from this wholeness, or separate from the bigger expanded container of who we are, to integrate into the wholeness of our true nature. We can start to listen and hear the needs of the split off parts of ourselves and then from the whole self we can gently give whatever is most needed that wasn't given at the time the part developed.

Over time it's about bringing all parts of us home, to our whole self. It can be helpful, if you're that way inclined, to have a sense of drawing on the strength of a spiritual figure like the Buddha or Jesus, a Goddess, or a spiritual presence that resonates with you. Perhaps a good spiritual teacher, coach or therapist might also be able to provide a level of modelling for your own potential to be whole, happy and free.

Summary ~ Step 8: Learning to Sustain Health and Wholeness

I invite you to learn to sustain your health by keeping up a self-care practice in your life even once you're fully well. To be aware of tendencies that may come back as you heal and to keep up your own personal growth and development. You are worth continuing to invest in your health and yourself, even as a fully healthy person, and to honour your changing needs. I also invite you to embrace your whole self: who is embodied, connected, courageous and present. From this place you can support others parts of yourself to feel nurtured and connected to who you truly are; and you can experience a deeply satisfying life.

Chapter 13
Summary: The Lotus Process

Now I've taken you through the 8 steps of The Lotus Process, here's a little recap on what you have learnt.

The 8 Steps of 'The Lotus Process'

Step 1: Acceptance and Surrender

The first stage of healing is to accept what is for now. The more you can let go into surrender and acceptance, and practice gratitude, will help you to build a strong foundation to support a health recovery path.

Step 2: Belief and Commitment

Belief is powerful to support you in physical healing, and committing to your path to wellbeing. You can heal chronic illness. YOU can do it. Keep going, and when you have doubt come up, work through it to get yourself back on track.

Step 3: Self-Care and Resources

If you take one thing away from this step, remember to look after yourself with compassion on a daily basis and follow your joy. I suggest you start with a morning meditation before breakfast, and use 'A Pause' as and when needed throughout the day. You might just choose one exercise from this step to embrace fully for now and integrate into your life, and come back when you are feeling the need for some fresh resources to support your healing. You are so worth resourcing yourself well.

Step 4: Community and Support

In this step we covered the value of a supportive community in the process of healing. You are so worth getting the external support and validation you deserve. Having a good community around you will help you navigate all the steps of The Lotus Process journey.

Step 5: Overcoming Blocks to Healing

This step is about getting clearer your personal inner blocks to recovery, and a sense of how to tenderly work with this important part of your healing path. We explore personality traits, unconscious blocks and secondary gains of illness; and how to overcome them.

Step 6: Purpose and Authenticity

Living your unique purpose in life, and following it with authenticity, is a key to moving towards the health you so deserve. Purpose can be big, or small and simple, it just has to be meaningful to you. It often helps if it is contributing to others of the world in some way. Being authentic is also about how you express yourself and show up in all areas of your life.

Step 7: Healing your Past

This step offers a sense of the process of healing emotional wounds and trauma from your body-mind system. It demonstrates the potential power of this process to support a deep and lasting health recovery, and to support you to move into a place of greater strength and resilience. Go gently and tenderly with this.

Step 8: Sustaining Health and Wholeness

This step is a vital step of learning to sustain your health, which will help you to stay in balance, and keep the health benefits you receive as you recover your health. Keep up a self-care practice in your life even once you're fully well. Be aware of tendencies that may come back as you heal and keep up your own personal growth and development. Continuing to invest in your health and yourself is a very worthwhile practice for the rest of your life. I also invite you to embrace your whole self: who is embodied, connected, courageous and present.

Chapter 14
Wishing you a Miraculous and Happy Life

"There are only two ways to live your life.

One is as though nothing is a miracle.

The other is as though everything is a miracle."

~Albert Einstein

Life is a miracle. The miraculous can be found in the simple day to day moments of living, as well as in the possibility to create deep and lasting healing from illness. Using the steps in this book, you can help to create the most optimal conditions for this kind of healing. Perhaps if we take really excellent care of ourselves, we can stay well into our nineties, a miracle and a real potential if we really practice the art of ongoing self-care and self-awareness.

If you follow all of the steps of The Lotus Process, it will help you to physically heal; be open to a miracle. Some steps might be more needed for your unique journey to health than others. Honour your own unique path to health and keep connecting to resources that most support you.

Life is also simple. We are here a while, we have great opportunities to create and be wonderful people. We die.

Coming back to the simplicity of this moment, the breath, can help us to appreciate the beautiful simplicity of our lives, and can bring us more in touch with who we really are.

Hold both: miraculous visions for yourself and the world; and the simplicity of 'being' fully here and now. In the miracle of this moment, of your body breathing, of the sounds of rain or the feeling of the sun on your skin.

Thank you for being here, and making it to the end of the book. I wish you well as you keep following these steps.

May you be filled with all the joy, health and happiness you deserve.

The Lotus Process Next Steps to Support you

Most people find they reach their health goals only when they have the support of a trusted mentor, therapist or coach. Someone to support you through the ups and downs, that you can be accountable to and with skills to help you navigate all the territories you might find yourself in.

Go to www.lotusprocess.com to access some free resources and to find out what your current next step with The Lotus Process could be at this time.

Appendix

EFT Introduction

One of my favourite methods for working with challenging emotions and holding patterns is Emotional Freedom Technique (EFT). EFT is an energy psychology approach that involves working on acupuncture points. Acupuncturists have been working on these points for thousands of years. EFT combines gentle tapping on acupuncture points with modern psychology tools to promote shifts in energy, mood and physical wellbeing.

Gary Craig, the founder, created an accessible and easy to apply modality that spread around the world, providing thousands with relief from physical, mental and emotional issues. One way of describing EFT could be psychological acupuncture without the needles. Another way could be a talk therapy that also involves working on the body. It is found to be a powerful modality to help resolve chronic health issues through releasing core issues beneath the physical symptoms and to support getting out of loops of stress that perpetuate illness cycles.

You stimulate energy meridian points on your body by tapping them with your fingertips whilst focusing on the problem, be it of an emotional or physical nature. The process is easy to memorise and can be done anywhere. The EFT Discovery Statement says "The cause of all negative emotions is an imbalance in the body's energy system."

Essentially meaning that energetic disturbance is the root of our emotional imbalances. It could also be said that, because our physical pains and diseases are often connected with our emotions, our unresolved negative emotions and the underlying energetic disturbance, are major contributors to most physical pains and diseases.

It is important to tune into the issue to indicate to your system what you are working with. The easiest way to do this is just to repeat the issue. You tap (around 7) times on specific points around the body, the purpose of which is to rebalance the energy system. You can use any two fingers, you don't need to tap on both sides and it's fine to alternate from one side to the other.

EFT Tapping Points

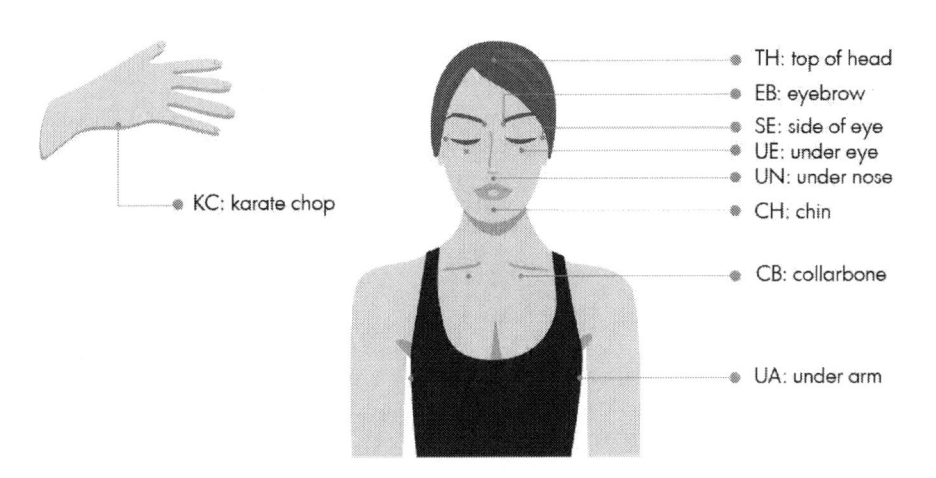

- KC: karate chop
- TH: top of head
- EB: eyebrow
- SE: side of eye
- UE: under eye
- UN: under nose
- CH: chin
- CB: collarbone
- UA: under arm

Chart courtesy of Gillian Morris Coaching (Designed by Love at home design)

To help heal chronic illness you can use EFT at every stage of The Lotus Process, for example:

Step 1) To address anything that gets in the way of an attitude of acceptance, surrender and gratitude, such as thoughts and fears about symptoms

Step 2) To address thoughts and fears about not recovering

Step 3) To release blocks to recovery such as personality traits that are holding back your healing or protective and fearful parts

Step 4) As a great resource to build inner strength and resilience

Step 5) To release issues that get in the way of happy secure relationships

Step 6) To overcome barriers to following your authentic purpose or being your authentic self

Step 7) To tap through and find relief from traumatic memories from the past

Step 8) To tap on the thoughts and emotions that come up if you're in a dip

The Basic EFT Process

1) Become aware of a physical symptom, emotion or belief you want to shift

2) Find a statement of acceptance of yourself with the issue e.g. 'Even though I have this sharp pain in my back and I feel frustrated with my body I accept myself anyway'

3) Tap the 'karate chop point' on the side of your hand three times while repeating the affirmation

4) Tap around all the points on the body while repeating what the issue is e.g. 'sharp pain in my back' and 'I feel frustrated'

To find out more about EFT please visit www.lotusprocess.com where you can find a resources PDF with links to videos to help you get the basics of this tool. For more in depth support with EFT my video programme of The Lotus Process or working with myself or another EFT practitioner is recommend.

The Enneagram

The idea of the Enneagram is that we all develop a fundamental personality type as a response to early wounding of some kind; some suggest we are born with it.

The core types are:

1 ~ The Reformer

2 ~ The Helper

3 ~ The Achiever

4 ~ The Individualist

5 ~ The Investigator

6 ~ The Loyalist

7 ~ The Enthusiast

8 ~ The Challenger

9 ~ The Peacemaker

Although we can't change our type, we can become highly functioning with it and we all have unique gifts to offer once we are integrated. So, for example, a peacemaker can become a great mediator. A helper learns the art of taking care of themselves and others from a place of resourcefulness.

As learning about the Enneagram and that I was a 'nine' or a 'peacemaker' was really helpful for my recovery journey, I am including a little about this in the appendix. I realised I had an underlying pattern of 'keep the peace at all costs, even to my health'. I would avoid conflict. I would numb out to avoid difficult feelings and circumstances. You can probably see how these tendencies can put stress on the nervous system and be part of the puzzle that leads to chronic illness.

Many clients have also found it revolutionary for understanding themselves and shifting some core patterns. My observations so far are that the clients I work with tend to be reformers, helpers, achievers, individualists, loyalists and peacemakers. If you're interested in exploring this more I would recommend the book 'The Wisdom of the Enneagram'[32].

---

[32] Don Richard Riso, R. Hudson. 1999 "*The Wisdom of the Enneagram: Complete Guide to Psychological and Spiritual Growth for the Nine Personality Types*" Bantan Books

My Full Recovery Story

My full story is adapted from a book of twelve recovery stories I co-wrote many years ago[33]. Prior to getting unwell in 2001 aged 19, I'd been travelling for a year. I taught English in Nepal for four months and then travelled around the world. I started at Nottingham University soon after my return home and in my first term at university I came down with what I later found out to be CFS/ME symptoms. Initially brain fog was my worst symptom, but gradually fatigue, muscle weakness, dizziness and headaches developed; I ended up having a constant headache for about six months.

I went back to university after the Christmas holidays to attempt my first term exams, but it was just too much; I was too ill and I was getting depressed about it. I couldn't stop crying, I was very scared and found studying impossible. I was told by a doctor at the university that it was likely to be depression. Although I knew that I was getting depressed, I knew also that I had something very physical going on and knew that it wasn't just depression. I didn't know what it was though, it felt very strange.

I was found to have low levels of iron in my body and was slightly anaemic, and this became my first hope of a cure. Really, I didn't think to be slightly anaemic would cause that severe symptoms but I did latch onto the prospect that iron tablets were going to cure me!

---

[33] Secrets to Recovery, 12 Lessons in Healing M.E./C.F.S./Fibromyalgia, Alex Howard, Anna Duschinsky and Frances Goodall

I ended up in a real mess physically and mentally for a few days, crying constantly with a sense of despair and helplessness. I was clearly unable to carry on at university. I had to go home to live with my mum and sister again, and it was very depressing at first. I'd spent a year independently travelling and two months at university and suddenly I'm back at home and unwell. I'd started to make some good friends at university and was really looking forward to getting to know them more. Initially, all of my school friends in Sheffield were away at University, so I felt quite lonely.

My sister was the first to actually mention the prospect of ME/CFS, although I'd never even heard of ME before. We were all scared about what it was and how serious or long term it could be. I was worried I might have a brain tumour as I had a constant headache in the early days. Thankfully after a brain scan I realised this wasn't what I'd got. When I found out what the symptoms of ME were, I did think that's what I'd got.

For a while, I was just at home struggling with the physical symptoms and emotionally down a lot of the time. I would spend a lot of time alone, with extreme fatigue, headaches and brain fog. Emotionally and mentally I felt very low much of the time too.

I watched some daytime television some early on and that was quite depressing. My life felt worthless and hopeless. I started doing relaxation tapes and that was a key early on, which started to give me some hope that I might be able to do something to help myself. I noticed the first time I did a relaxation tape my headaches lessened considerable, my brain felt a bit clearer and I had more energy. It was an obvious sign that my body and mind really needed to relax more.

After a couple of months of feeling helpless at home, I was very glad to discover that a Buddhist Centre had just moved around the corner from my house. I started to go to meditate there most days, and early on this was the only activity I could manage outside the house. I also started to do daily meditation at home. I got interested in meditation before being unwell when I was in Nepal; reading about it, making Buddhist friends and dipping into a little meditation practice.

I found peace when I was doing meditation, and this was such a support. I also began a yoga class and started doing some yoga at home too, and together they began to help me feel I had ways I could help myself. The Buddhist philosophy of acceptance of things as they are, and a process of learning through the suffering which is inherent in being human, was very powerful to keep coming back to.

I read many books on Buddhism in the early stages of being ill and felt supported by the philosophy, also to feel that this time of being unwell may be a great opportunity to practice spiritually, to help me grow in wisdom and compassion. At moments when I was doing my meditation or yoga I could even start to see it as a blessing and experience a deeper sense of peace and wholeness. Although I'd then come back to the reality of my situation and it would be really difficult at times. Overall, though, I felt that I was starting a process of spiritual development that would benefit me for my whole life.

I had a two-year period of being ill and I felt in the same brain foggy cloud almost the whole time, except for little windows of better health and wellbeing during or after meditation, yoga or relaxation. Generally, I felt that my poor concentration and brain fog was one of the worst symptoms and most difficult to find much relief from. I found certain situations difficult to deal with, like social situations. My brain couldn't handle talking to lots of people or people talking across each other. I used to get really upset sometimes, I'd try and go out to socialise and end up in tears because I couldn't cope with it and had to go home.

I also regularly had nightmares and experienced sleep paralysis, where I was somewhere between sleep and awake and couldn't move. This was pretty terrifying, especially when it often involved a dream of a dark figure in bed with me that wasn't supposed to be there.

I had some Homeopathy through the NHS with a really kind Buddhist Homeopath. Combined with meditation and yoga practice, changing my diet and falling in love, after two years I got much better for a while and actually thought I was cured.

Around this time, I had a peak experience in meditation, which was very intense and left me feeling high for two weeks, hardly able to sleep and overflowing with energy. In a way, it was quite an intense initial 'awakening' experience, which affected the undercurrent of my being thereafter. Later I attributed this experience to the rising of kundalini energy: spiritual energy stored at the base of the spine that facilitates spiritual growth. At the time this happened I was doing a loving-kindness meditation where we were being led to bring the Buddha of compassion, Amitabha, within. I suddenly felt merged with a transcendental state of consciousness and enjoyed a blissful and deeply healing state of being.

It was amazing to feel so much energy; I naively thought I was cured of ME/CFS. It was also a little disconcerting that I felt so high - surely it wasn't natural to feel this high all the time? The whole experience was heightened by the fact that I was falling in love with a man I ended up entering a relationship with, a meditation teacher who I had on a spiritual pedestal.

The high settled down and for a while afterwards I felt considerably better physically and mentally. Yet a few weeks later I was just about to start my second term at University (my second attempt), and my health crashed. This time I felt worse than I ever had before, I could hardly walk, manage to look after myself and felt so weak it terrified me.

I had to lie down much of the time for six weeks. I was forced to leave my University course for the second time. I did improve again, and entered a boom and bust cycle that lasted for nearly three years, although was gradually improving throughout this time. I feel the extremes I felt in this time ranging from feeling 'cured' to feeling flat out ill were in part a result of the kundalini energy on a body and mind that weren't properly prepared.

In that period a friend gave me a Reiki treatment. I felt that lifted a lot of emotional things that were going on around being ill and was quite amazed by how much better that made me feel. I ended up learning Reiki level one and two and did about an hour a day of Reiki on myself for a year, which I found very beneficial.

Through my Reiki teacher I found out about Bowen therapy and decided to train, once I got to the point where I was well enough to take the training course. Bowen therapy is a gentle form of body therapy, gentle rolling movements are made over muscles to stimulate the body to rebalance and heal itself. It is often used for muscular-skeletal problems, but it can be used for releasing tension and improving energy levels with Chronic Fatigue.

Certainly, as I was training I was amazed at how much I could manage, the first part of the course was four full days but I felt better after than I did before I went. Many people commented on how tight my muscles were. It was clear to me that beginning to release that tension was going to free up energy. To manage four full days was a surprising indicator of what I could actually manage, as opposed to what I thought; I completely expected that it would wear me out but in fact, it had quite the opposite effect.

I knew people in Sheffield who were practicing Bowen and we were doing swaps. It was definitely helping my health to improve, quite significantly at times; although it wasn't addressing some of the underlying patterns that were keeping me ill. I think it was good in that it was improving my energy levels and making me realise the potential my body had for being well. At the time, I wasn't yet resolving the underlying issues that were causing me to relapse again and again.

Although on reflection I don't think it was always that I was doing something 'wrong' that was making me ill again; the process of healing is often up and down. I also believe there were natural cycles happening as I was going through the process of kundalini rising. People often get Chronic Fatigue symptoms while undergoing this process. I feel perhaps the illness for me was related to lots of blocked energy in my body-mind-energy system. When I started meditating aged 18 it started the kundalini process which was part of what floored me with ME/CFS. I had many things to work out and change in myself. I know I had many of the ME personality tendencies such as a perfectionist, helper and achiever.

I had a very strong pattern of feeling well and thinking I was cured and almost forgetting how ill I'd been and doing too much, that was the boom and bust cycle which essentially went on for three years. I would do crazy things like suddenly going out and thinking I could run having been lying on the sofa for a week barely able to move; hoping I might be able to run off the remains of the illness!

At times in the final 3 years of the illness, I was so well. I danced for a whole weekend of 5 Rhythms, a movement meditation I loved. I became well enough to go to China to see my mum and her partner who were teaching there, which was great. I walked the furthest I had since being unwell and also went on a day cycle ride; however, other times, I had to spend a few days in bed feeling unwell and unhappy again.

Each time I felt more ill there was a lot of blame and criticism towards myself. Yet once I managed to let go of the criticism, and accept and surrender to the situation as it was, I would pick up again and surprisingly quickly the symptoms would often again lift. I also read with relief that the process of recovery was an up and down one, and that was quite natural, which took away some of my inner critic when I was down and also helped me to trust it didn't mean I had gone right back or would never recover. I was in a process of recovery, and it helped me to know and trust that.

In the last year of my recovery I also read The Journey by Brandon Bays and ended up attending her workshop, which I found very healing. I felt so drawn to this way of working that I booked on the next course. I was desperate to be completely healed. I was also using her approach in meditation and going into intense emotional states, and dropping through to peace beneath. From deepening these experiences, I also able to be with whatever was present in each moment and allow it to be there. Surrendering and letting go in the present.

Around this time, I began to get jolts in my meditation practice as the energy that was now very active in my system hit a block in the area of my diaphragm. One of the traumas from which I healed from as I got better was a severe physical attack as a teenager, which came up in a very intense way initially with the journey work. So intensely, that it possibly could've been seen as re-traumatising, but over time addressing this trauma in various ways was important to my healing journey.

I regularly used mindfulness to help me to calm my thinking down by coming back to the moment and my body. This helped my body be in a good state to heal. At the time I had also just got into a therapy that views CFS as very linked to emotions. I started to see a pattern of the clear links with my emotions and symptoms. I remember having an evening of feeling unwell yet sure I'd found the final key to unlocking the illness and I felt quite excited.

In one of my sessions it came up clearly that my way of dealing with my emotions and not feeling able to deal with conflict with others, was a key to my symptoms and being able to overcome them. I realised my remaining symptoms and illness, was a message that I wasn't responding to my emotions and I needed to respond more clearly to them. That was things like not being passive in situations and saying something if it needs to be said, rather than putting it off.

I was towards the end of the illness and it was just amazing. I felt much better after the first treatment just knowing what I needed to say to a couple of people. I felt empowered by it and actually felt that it was the final key to being well. I ended up expressing anger and actually being quite aggressive, but it seemed I had to do that to become more balanced. I was moving towards the middle way, not being passive and not being aggressive. I did go to the aggressive temporarily and it was helping my health to be more authentic with my feelings but I know if it was not entirely positive as a long-term way of relating to people.

Like a pendulum, I was too far one way, and swung too far the other way, in order to come back into balance again. In Marshall Rosenburg's book on NVC 'A Language of Life', he talks about how if we have been people pleasers we need to go through an obnoxious phase in order to come back into balance, where we recognise the importance of our needs and other people's needs in a healthy balance.

At Brandon Bay's second weekend, 'Manifest Abundance', I allowed myself to completely surrender to the universe, praying to be completely healed and free and able to get on with my life. A past trauma strongly came up as needing to be healed. I came back feeling spiritually transformed but strangely inhuman; I felt the deep love I had for my boyfriend of two years had dissolved, which led to a separation.

I felt lost after this: far too spiritually open and unable to contain my experience. At times I remember feeling weak in my body, and like I was dissolving and disappearing. Yet I did have energy more often than not, and was also in the process of beginning work after a long time on the sick.

On my good days this was fine; at other times I really struggled with physical symptoms and an intense, open state of consciousness. It wasn't helped that my first part-time job to run alongside developing therapy work was in an after school club, and suddenly after what had in some ways felt like a four-and-a-half-year retreat, I was surrounded by loads of loud children! I didn't last long in this job and soon focused solely on my therapy work. I varied between extremes of energy, clarity, health and happiness, and fatigue, fear, depression and doubt.

At times I felt like I didn't exist, I had to pinch myself to remind myself I was actually here. I had out of body experiences while lying in bed going to sleep, like I was rising up out of my body and may never come back. On walking out in the woods once I heard a beautiful harmonic sound and stopped in awe. My body jolted in meditation as I felt the energy meet a block in my solar plexus and random sounds came out of my mouth- sometimes shock like sounds and occasionally more harmonic sounds. I had an involuntary muscle spasm in my tongue which made a clicking sound. I felt like I was balancing on the edge with enlightenment on one side and insanity on the other and felt a lot of fear as a result. Clearly these weren't 'normal' experiences! Although they can be quite normal for someone undergoing a kundalini awakening, I later discovered.

I got into one of the worst lows I had ever been in, like I was in a dark strange terrifying black hole which I couldn't escape from. The light was there in the periphery, but I felt in the darkness and couldn't escape. I was experiencing a lot of fear and also feeling fatigued and ill.

Fortunately, exactly at this time a friend had printed some stuff off the internet which he felt to be very relevant to me.

Being mystified at my insistence that it was no longer good for me to meditate he researched why this could be so. I read with relief about kundalini energy and the problems it can bring up as well as the ineffable transcendental states of consciousness.

Yet reading some of the articles only provoked more fear, reading about people ending up on anti-psychotics and suffering physical and mental difficulties for years afterwards. I felt I had veered off my healing and spiritual path into a darkness I couldn't escape from and had times of feeling there was no point in going on. Yet this would clear and a clarity, peace and acceptance would come again; like another level of my consciousness was being cleared, to leave peace and relief. I completely stopped meditating, focused on developing my therapy business and doing positive things. I began regular exercise; swimming, running and walking. My task now seemed to be to integrate the experience in to my life and being.

It is conceivable to me though that the whole illness may be attributed to my body being too dense with trapped energy and emotion, that when I began to open myself spiritually, my body shut down. I'd actually begun meditation practice just before getting unwell.

As though it was clear I had a lot of healing to do before I could open myself to spiritual development, and the illness was the way my body would force me to do this. Furthermore, in my daily life I never stopped 'doing' in an unhealthy way and so there was a huge divide between my newly formed Buddhist meditation practice, an interest that began the year before while on my Gap Year in Nepal, and the way I was living my life.

I was 19 when I got CFS/ME, and 21 when I had my initial 'awakening' experience so it's not surprising I suffered the difficulties I have. I entered CFS/ ME after some chaotic teenage years of alcohol and drugs, and was taken on a journey of healing and transformation. I now see it is important to ideally have the roots right before one goes too deeply into spiritual practice: to be functional in the world, to have a job, healthy relationships and be in a healthy environment. Yet despite all the problems this energy caused within me, paradoxically I feel it was a central part of my healing. I had experiences of waking up in the night with the sensation that healing light was just pouring through me, each time I hoped I would wake up fully cured.

I write quite a lot about the spiritual emergence side to my ME/CFS journey because it is a little known phenomenon, especially the difficulties it can cause. Possibly to inspire fellow seekers, while also warning of caution when seeking spiritual transformation and to provide insight to other people who may be undergoing a similar experience. I'm also interested that sometimes ME/CFS symptoms can be linked to this process, and that even if it's not in your case, there is learning from both angles. In that, carefully managed, a spiritual awakening can facilitate physical healing, and that physical illness can be a part of the process of an awakening. I propose that viewing an illness as an invitation for a spiritual initiation is an empowering and positive way of framing the experience. I also believe that a lot of the time, it's true.

I was grateful to meet someone on a retreat I worked on who had undergone similar spiritual experiences and to talk to people with a lot of experience of meditation about everything. It gradually all settled down, and now for a decade I have felt much more balanced and grateful for the journey ill health and spiritual development took me on.

During my healing process from CFS I was found to have pre-cancerous cells on my cervix. After a few years I was advised that I needed laser treatment on them. I asked them to give me six months to see if I could heal them myself. I continued with all my healing practices and added healing visualisations around my cervix, such as visualising healing light flowing through. Six months later they were gone and when I went back for check-ups I became known as 'the self-healing woman'.

Eventually aged 23 I considered myself cured of ME/CFS. I found attending a course that combined NLP, Hypnotherapy, EFT and Coaching helpful in this process of integration of the journey and getting back into life post-ME/CFS and the spiritual emergence I went through. This also gave me skills to add to my profession in holistic healthcare and wellness.

I love my work as a therapist, working both one to one with clients and in a group setting, and being able to contribute to other's journeys to health. I work now predominantly with people with ME/CFS, ME and FMS in my one to one practice. Through Women's Wellness Circle, in online and in-person group programmes, we attract women with a variety of chronic physical health conditions who have found relief from a range of symptoms such as endometriosis, healing post-surgery and migraines.

My secrets to my eventual full recovery were learning to respond to my emotions, clearing old emotions and following a spiritual path, yet learning to trust once it felt it had all gone terribly wrong! To learn again and again to come back to the present moment and to accept however that was, that through acceptance things would naturally start to shift, but resistance would keep the situation locked in place.

You can recover, begin to believe you can and take positive action to help you get there! It will likely require some financial investment and commitment to practicing what you learn, but in the end you can get there and it will have been so worth it.

Now I'm no longer seeking 'awakening', only to continue the life work of moving to deeper levels of freedom, happiness, embodiment and wholeness. To live in the moment, and to integrate more fully the spiritual awareness into all areas of my life. That it may assist me in being of better service to others and the world.

In the years since being well I have loved developing my work and life to a place where I am very happy with it. I have now thousands of hours of client experience. I have specialised in using EFT (Emotional Freedom Techniques) and being an Amygdala Retraining Coach to help people recover from Chronic Fatigue and related conditions. Many years ago I started running residential retreats with a friend and colleague, Sophie, focusing on the themes of Recovering Wellbeing and Women's Circles. Now we are known as Women's Wellness Circle and offer retreats and online programmes for wellbeing.

I built up my fitness to run a half marathon in 2012, and another in 2015. I love going running, especially out in the Peak District when I get the chance. I'm glad to be back writing this book, something I started a few years ago and dreamed of for many years before that.

In 2011 I met my partner, Paul, and we had a child in 2013, who is 3 at the time of writing. My family are such a joy to me alongside my joy and passion of my work, friends and running. I am in deep gratitude to my relationship. Of course we have ups and downs, but finding someone who is willing to stand back and take responsibility and where we can create sacred space to share openly from our hearts and resolve any issues that arise. Feeling deeply called to have a child as well, who has been such a delight to bring into the world. There is a flow of love a lot of the time and I couldn't ask for more.

In the decade of being well I have continued with deep exploration of my own inner healing; in part to ensure my own inner container for clients expands and deepens. This means I can offer a deeper level of healing, exploration and growth. I know it supports me in my relationships, work, my mothering and being happy.

A passion in recent years is ancestral healing, where emotional and energetic blockages in my system have taken me back to ancestors unhealed pain. I have done this both on my own and in personal sessions, being guided back to ancestral trauma. Indeed, there is quite obvious trauma in my lineage with my grandfather's family killed in the holocaust. For example, a pain in my pelvis took me back to my great grandmother who was killed in Auschwitz, and a blocked area in my spine guided me back to my grandfather and the pain he carried as a result of losing his parents aged 16.

Using an awareness of the family constellations approach with EFT (Emotional Freedom Technique) to help the feelings move through and clear. Since doing this I have felt deeply held fear patterns dropping away leaving greater levels of calm and freedom in my body-mind system. Many years of PMS started to drop away as I did this deeper work.

For the last year or so, after doing some training and getting supervision in constellations, I have been bringing this level of work more consciously and clearly into my work with clients as well.

Who knows where life unfolds from here, I'll keep flowing with life and the people I meet on the journey. I love how in my work I have collaborated with different people along the way, and all have taught me. I seem to work best working in partnership with others; it seems to be my nature. For instance, I am passionate about working with groups of women, and my work with Sophie feeds a deep part of me, as well as being a support for the community of women involved.

I feel I am called to offer myself in bigger ways to the world, so may this book be a part of that offering. I have brought together my personal experience of healing, combined with thousands of hours of client experiences, to create The Lotus Process. My longing is that this spreads out into the world and helps many people on their path to physical healing. May you be one of those people.

'From housebound with chronic health issues to running i'd love to support you on your journey to wellness'

Recommended Resources

Of course there are many great resources out there, a selection with my websites and some of my favourite websites and books are below:

Websites

To download The Lotus Process resources PDF and be in touch with me: www.lotusprocess.com

Women's Wellness Circle for online courses and retreats for women: www.womenswellnesscircle.com

The Wholeness Process: www.wholenessprocess.org

High quality EFT resources: www.tappingqanda.com and https://efthelps.com

Awakening Women Institute: www.awakeningwomen.com

Mankind Project: www.mankindproject.org

Tantra teachers: www.janday.com and www.jewelswingfield.com

The Red School (menstrual cycle support): www.redschool.net

Books

Belonging Here: A Guide for the Spiritually Sensitive, *Judith Blackstone*

Even if it cost me my Life: Systematic Constellations and Serious Illness- *Stephan Hausner*

Feeling Safe - *William Bloom*

Grace and Grit - *Ken Wilber*

Loving What Is: Four Questions that Can Change your Life - *Byron Katie*

Non-Violent Communication: A Language of Life - Marshall Rosenburg

Scared Sick: The Role of Childhood Trauma in Adult Disease - *Robin Karr-Morse with Meredith S.Wile*

Tantra: Discover the Path from Sex to Spirit - *Shashi Solluna*

The Journey - *Brandon Bays*

The Power of Now - *Echkart Tolle*

The Spiritual Dimension of the Enneagram - *Sandra Maitri*

Waking the Tiger - *Peter Levine*

Trauma and Memory - *Peter Levine*

The Wisdom of the Enneagram - *Don Richard Riso and R. Hudson*

The Optimized Woman - *Miranda Gray*

The Art of Sexual Ecstasy - *Margot Anand*

Why I am Sick - *Richard Flook*

About the Author

Frances Goodall is a Wellbeing Coach who draws on over sixteen years of training and experience in the area of health and wellbeing, and personal and spiritual development. Her work is influenced from her own experience of healing from CFS/ME 2001-2006 and a decade helping others to heal from chronic illnesses as a bodyworker, coach and psychology practitioner. Frances is passionate about helping others to achieve their health goals and to awaken to their true potential as they physically heal.

Frances is also an EFT Trainer and the co-founder of Women's Wellness Circle. You can find out more about everything Frances currently offers at www.francesgoodall.com